# MARK OF THE BEAST

ALESIA T. WILLIAMS

CREATION HOUSE
A STRANG COMPANY

MARK OF THE BEAST by Alesia Williams
Published by Creation House
A Strang Company
600 Rinehart Road
Lake Mary, Florida 32746
www.strangbookgroup.com

This book or parts thereof may not be reproduced in any form, stored in a retrieval system, or transmitted in any form by any means—electronic, mechanical, photocopy, recording, or otherwise—without prior written permission of the publisher, except as provided by United States of America copyright law.

All Greek and Hebrew words are taken from *The New Strong's Exhaustive Concordance* of the Bible published by James Strong, L.L.D., S.T.D., and used by permission of Thomas Nelson, Inc.

All Scripture passages are taken from The King James Version of the Bible.

Publisher's Note: The views expressed in this book are not necessarily the views held by the publisher.

Design Director: Bill Johnson
Cover design by Justin Evans

Copyright © 2009 by Alesia Williams
All rights reserved

Library of Congress Control Number: 2009936775
International Standard Book Number: 978-1-59979-947-6

First Edition

09 10 11 12 13 — 9 8 7 6 5 4 3 2 1
Printed in the United States of America

I dedicate this book to my husband, an apostle and my only friend. Thank you for your faithfulness to God and our home. You are indeed a man of God, a faithful servant, strong warrior, and weight bearer. Thank you for not collapsing. Thank you for persevering. Thank you for all your support. Thank you for allowing your heart to be transformed. This is the heart cry of God. It is the Spirit of the Father inside of a man. His heart cries, "Teach me how to love You!"

# CONTENTS

1 Is Your Marriage Cursed?.................... 1

2 The Pudenda and the Heart.................... 23

3 Two Thieves and a Yardstick.................... 43

4 The Two Towers.................... 67

5 I Don't Feel Like a Man in My Own House.......... 85

6 Throwing the Baby Out with the Bath Water.................... 103

7 There's a Lion in the House and He Must Go!.................... 109

Chapter 1

# IS YOUR MARRIAGE CURSED?

FROM THE DAY Adam sinned to the present, God has been seeking someone that He could give His mind to. The kingdom of heaven has suffered violence, and the spirit of Jezebel is running rampant. Many believe that she is a woman wearing makeup and a red dress. Throughout this book, I will show you how the spirit of Jezebel once lived inside Dagon. He is the fish god the Philistines worshiped.

When man refuses God's plan, demons that were pulled out of their ranks regain their positions. This allows that spirit to take on a new name and become more progressive in someone else. In Matthew 8:20, Jesus said, "The foxes have holes, and the birds of the air *have* nests; but the Son of man hath not where to lay *his* head" (emphasis added).

The Greek word for head is *kephale* (kef-al-ay). The head is the part most readily taken hold of, particularly in war. The *Strong's* reference number for the word *head* is 2776.

Ever since Adam failed, mankind has not fully taken

on the mind of God. This has left God without a place to lay His head. As quoted from Matthew 8:20, the foxes have a hole, and the birds of the air have a nest, but God has no one to whom He can give His mind. He has no one who would stop being selfish, so that He can live in his body without that person getting in His way. This is why marriages fail. It is impossible to fight to the victory when the man in authority is operating in his own mind, disobedient to the will of God. To make matters worse, the man who is supposed to cover his wife has become Satan's assassin because he is greedy, just like Adam.

Throughout this book, I will show you the power of the hands. The first woman tore down her house because she did not wait on the man. Her greed changed God's plan forever. God gave us Christ to restore mankind. The authority of God is now being abused. Women must understand the power they have to change a man forever. Men must understand their position to cover and correct a woman who is being attacked by the serpent spirit. Together they must help each other. This means both must fully understand what God expects out of the marriage. Afterward, you must make up your mind to do it. This raises one question. What does God really want?

Ephesians 5:23 states the husband is the head of the wife, even as Christ is the Head of the church and the Savior of the body. As in the earlier Scripture passage, the Greek word for head in this verse is *kephale*. When a man allows Satan to take him captive, he cannot guard his bride the way Christ guards the church. This is why many women are sick. A man is supposed to cover his wife the way God's Spirit covers them both. Then they are supposed to help each other and rely on the Word of God. This will establish God's order in the home the way God wanted it to be in the beginning. They both must understand that they belong to God. He expects both of them to submit to His will and be covered by His Word. This cannot happen if lust and greed enters the covenant. The revelation of submission is deeper than both of them submitting to Christ.

In the beginning God made man the head. He is supposed to cover the woman. She is a picture of the church. The forbidden fruit belonged to God. It was up to Adam to speak into the woman's life. Adam failed to do that. The woman fell into lust and greed. Adam agreed with her disorder and as a result, mankind has not taken on the mind of God. The authority of God has been abused. Men and women have hurt one another.

God wants men to operate with His mind. Men must die to selfishness. Most of all men must present their bodies as a living sacrifice. This empowers them to tell the devil, "It is finished. I am through with being greedy. I am done with agreeing with disorder. I will protect my wife from being attacked by the serpent of lust. I will not condone anything that God forbids." This mindset then empowers the man to become a picture of Christ. The man willingly presents his body to God. God's Spirit will rest in the man. The man will have the heart of a father and not a serpent. The woman will be covered and led. If a man agrees with lust and selfishness, he will do exactly what Adam did. This means that he will sow to his flesh and reap corruption. This raises two questions: What does it mean to sow to your flesh? And, what does it mean to reap corruption? The answers, which are discussed in a later chapter, reveal what kind of government came as a result of the first family. It shows how a government becomes divided when two people fall into lust.

In the day of Adam, man had power over the beast, Satan. This can be seen in Adam and Eve's treading on the serpent. But, greed caused man to be attacked by the beast. This is seen in Cain's murder of Abel after their father fell into lust. The serpent represents the beast, which is an unclean spirit. It needed a body to operate through.

Eating the forbidden fruit released the devourer, Satan. He would use mankind to devour and kill each other. The beast would live in mankind, and mankind would live a life of whoredom. Satan would use them to murder each other. This is the outcome of the family and the human body. It will always be attacked when the head of the house falls into lust. It is also the outcome of any nation when God has been locked out. There will be vicious attacks such as by wind and water.

Satan has always attacked the head. This includes the mind, men, and Christ. When one does not have knowledge of the Word, he cannot stand. This is why the beast attacks the mind. The male is considered to be the head of the family. This is why Satan attacks men. He made sure that many of them would not be fathered properly. He wants them to pass their pains to their children while in the house with them.

Christ is the Head. He is also the anointing that God put in a body. God judged Christ for the sins of mankind. This was a great act of faith. Man can now freely come to God. Christ is the example God used to show men how to live when one claims God as his Father.

Matthew 14:8, "And she, being before instructed of her mother, said, Give me here John Baptist's head in a charger." Notice the word *head* in this verse.

God declared the kingdom must come. It cannot happen when our heads are on the devil's platter. It does not matter if it is a man or a woman being used by Satan. Satan already has their heads on his plate even though he is using one of them to behead someone else.

In Matthew 14, John cried out against Herod's adulterous affair. He stated that it was unlawful for Herod to have his brother's wife. Herod became angry, and his wife stood in agreement with him. They had John imprisoned. Herod did not want to kill John. He only wanted to lock him away and silence him. This reminds me of the church, which has put the voice of God out of its house.

Rebellion always leads to destruction. Satan will use whatever one gives place to. Rebellion opens the door for the devil to kill the person who was only meant to be locked away. In the natural realm, it looked like the man of God was imprisoned. However, in the spirit realm, it was a declaration that God had been locked out of His own house. The voice of God was in a prison. This meant the people had no Voice to speak to them.

This reminds me of a man with children who has been locked out of his house. That man is deprived of his rights to be a father. Those in the house want him to pay the bills and keep up the payments, but they want to run the house.

The serpent spirit has wrecked God's house. The church is out of order. Our relationships are out of order. This goes back to the garden. The serpent is working through the flesh. This is why men are not honored in their own homes. They will not be so honored until God is honored first.

Everything that has happened in our homes has already happened in the church. Our society and our homes are a manifestation of what is heard from the pulpit. Building a pulpit with your own message will pollute the church, our homes, and society.

In the fourteenth chapter of Matthew, Herod's wife told her daughter to ask for John's head on a charger. Herod was sad and never intended for things to get out of hand with the beheading of John.

In the natural realm, it looked like a man was assassinated while imprisoned. In the spirit realm, it was a declaration that the voice of God has been murdered. This is the result of being cunning, manipulative, selfish, lustful, and greedy. These characteristics exist both in society and in the church. In the garden, the first family became greedy. They ate the forbidden fruit. The serpent spirit was given authority. This is the flesh operating without God. The first thing the serpent claimed was the government.

Eating the forbidden fruit divided the family. It caused the church and the government to be separated. One man plus one woman equals one government. One man plus one woman equals one church. One man plus one woman equals divine apostolic order. One man plus one woman equals one pulpit. One man plus one woman equals one house. One man plus one woman equals one tower. The first man and woman is a picture of one government. They represent an image of one church, one pulpit, and one tower. In the beginning the church and the government are one.

Greed for God's portion released the devourer, the seedeater. Selfishness took the first family out of the presence of God. The snake fight will begin, in which the serpent spirit operates through people. As time progresses, we will see the snake manifest itself in humanity, specifically the government. This is pharaoh in authority. He has no respect for praying women. He wants women to kill male babies. This is also the serpent spirit operating in a man. The serpent spirit is trying to mislead women. It is a picture of a man with authority over a woman. She is being led away from God. The serpent spirit is working through the man in authority. Only God knows what a government will do to her womb when her man leaves her. She will abort her children. Everything ungodly will become legal.

The government is a picture of a woman that has many children and no fathers for them. She despises God because the serpent spirit is strangling her. This is the outcome of the family and nation when a man does not stand up for God. We can expect this in the kingdoms of this world, when a man goes along with the lust of a woman. The serpent will use men and women to hurt each other and God.

Our homes are filled with lust and greed. We have produced disorderly children who hate God. This disorder entered in through the first family. We have become so lustful that God has no place to lay His head.

Keep in mind that the first family fell into lust. God gave us Christ. This sacrifice brought God's government back to Him. It will be up to men and women to submit to God. This means husbands and wives must help each other. Men and women must stop operating with the mind of the serpent. A man must name a woman and speak God's destiny for her into her life. In the beginning, Adam failed to do that. He named the woman after she sinned, but he never corrected her in love. He agreed with the serpent that pulled her away from him and God. But, God ordained their marriage when the Spirit of the Father brought the woman to the man. Adam was supposed to speak to her the will of God for her life. He stood right there, but did not open his mouth.

The same thing is happening today. Many women are left to seek God on their own. Their husbands are without vision. Wives are listening to every voice that sounds like God, but nobody told men that God put them in authority. When He did, it was not for men to agree with disorder. Neither do men have a right to lead their wives away from God. This means we, as believers, must find out what the forbidden fruit is.

The first woman is a picture of the church. The man represents God's image. God's Spirit is given a shape and a form. God's Spirit needed a body through which to operate. Man is the face of God. God's face was on the waters on the first day of Creation. God called His image out of the ground on the sixth day of Creation, but greed for the forbidden fruit destroyed the image of God.

This is the beginning of many kingdoms. Humanity will have as many husbands and wives as they want. Nobody will understand that the spirit of the lion entered in when Adam sinned. This is the beginning of two spirits, two governments, and two houses. Men and women will be married, but they do not live together. They will love each other, but remain inconsiderate. They will divorce and marry someone else, and then they will remarry husband number five after divorcing their ninth husband.

The serpent of lust is after all of us. This disorder goes back to the garden. The woman became greedy. The man agreed with it. The serpent of deception entered in. The image of God was destroyed. God's image could be seen in the waters on the first day of Creation. God's image could also be seen in the ground. What face do you see in the ground now? I will answer this question in the last chapter. It will reveal the power of a woman's hands.

Please do not feel bad. I am not here to beat you up. God spoke to me around the end of 2005. He told me that many peoples' houses are on fire. Then He said nobody would come out alive, except Him. God is after His purpose. The shaking and the crushing have begun. God wants one house. He wants one body. God is calling for one family.

The greed of Adam and Eve released division of all kinds. This includes denominations, divorce, and racism. The list goes on. Humanity is so lustful that it wants nothing to do with order. Disorder is the spirit of the serpent and the lion. In this next scripture, I will show you the power of the serpent and the lion. The serpent twists the mind. It is a picture of the beast that was in the garden. This spirit wanted the woman. It needed the man's permission. When Adam agreed with the woman's disorder, his agreement released the spirit of strangulation. A woman has to allow the man to deal with the serpent spirit. Adam was supposed to rebuke the serpent. Instead he assisted it. This left God's Spirit without a body to operate through.

Psalm 91:13 says, "Thou *shalt* tread upon the lion and adder: the young lion and the dragon *shalt* thou trample under feet" (emphasis added). This reveals the spirit of the beast. These are animalistic spirits that live in people. The first one is the adder. An adder is a smallish snake. Its nature is to kill, and as such some species of the adder are quite poisonous. In general, not all snakes are venomous. Nevertheless, the bite from one can still cause severe pain.

The snake was in the garden with Adam and Eve. His goal was to afflict both of them. He understands the power they have as a team. He is a spirit that needs to infiltrate both of them. This beast cannot operate without a body.

The snake is an animal. God knew the nature of this beast. The enemy could not release deadly venom without their permission. The snake needed to get Adam and Eve to eat something that God had told them they could not have. Let's look deeper into the word *adder*. Please keep in mind we are talking about the nature of a snake.

The Hebrew word for adder is *pethen* (peh-then), meaning "to twist, wind, or bend." The *Strong's* reference number for *adder* is 6620.

The word *twist* means "to wrap one thing around something else." It also means "to disturb mentally and confuse emotionally in order to breakdown." The twisting process is always used for two purposes. The first is to change something from its original form. The second is to make it take on the image of the thing that is twisting or wrapping itself around it. This is the nature of the serpent. He was present in the garden. Adam and Eve had the ability to tread on this beast. His spirit is unclean. His goal is to attack the woman. He twisted her mind with his words. This was designed to confuse her. Satan understands the emotions of the female. He must get her to ignore what Adam tells her. If not, then the snake must make sure the husband fails to tell the wife what God says. When all else fails, the snake must get the man to agree with the woman. It did not matter to the serpent if the woman was warned or not. He just needed Adam to agree with it.

As you know, the woman ate the forbidden fruit. Adam was standing right there when she did it, and she offered some to him and he ate it. (See Genesis 3:6.)

Adam is the strength that the woman needed. Adam ruled over the snake before God gave him a wife. Adam proved to have the heart of his Father. Adam walked in the image of his Father. Adam denied himself in the presence of a tree whose fruit looked delicious. He proved himself to be disciplined. This qualified him to have a wife. It empowered him to operate like his Father.

His Father's Spirit will rule the nations of the world. His Father's Spirit will rule his house. Adam's body is the Father's temple. The forbidden fruit will determine what spirit will run the nation and Adam's house. This raises a question: How important is the woman's role in the family? I believe the woman's role in the family reveals the unity of a husband and a wife. She is a picture of Adam's inner body. The serpent is a picture of lust; he is the destroyer. Agreeing with a woman's lust will break a man down from the inside out. Only God knows what a man does when he is without God and without his wife.

The woman is the foundation of the family. She determines the destiny of the household. She signifies stability for the man. It is not good for him to be alone. He needs her support. She desperately needs him. The two must help each other. He must cover and instruct her. She is strong, yet vulnerable. She is powerful only because she came out of God's image. Her life and submission determine what spirit will rule. Her response will be a picture of what is going on in Adam. If he agrees, it is a sign that he will fall in love with his flesh. This means he must stand against her disorder and correct her in love. He must respond the way God requires. The man must represent God without wavering.

As you know, Adam agreed with Eve. The serpent spirit stepped in. This is the beginning of deception. The woman is allowed to walk in disorder. She was never corrected. The man valued his own opinion. He walked in pride. Deception and pride are the nature of Satan. The fatherhood of God never manifested. This takes me to the nature of the lion.

Satan is as a roaring lion. I will show you how his spirit operates in a government. The lion stepped on to the globe when the first family sinned. Keep in mind, Adam and Eve are a picture of one government. This is what happens to the family and a nation when two people become greedy. This is the outcome of God's government when the spirit of the lion gets between two people. Psalm 91:13 remains pertinent to this discussion, "Thou shalt tread upon the *lion* and adder: the young *lion* and the dragon shalt thou trample under feet" (emphasis added). Notice the word *lion* appears twice. The Hebrew word for young lion reveals the cruel nature of Satan working through people.

As a young lion, this spirit is not mature. This is the beast operating in Adam and Eve. They became deceived, proud, and greedy. The beast did not use them to kill each other physically. Nevertheless, the two of them became disconnected from God. Eventually this young lion spirit reaches maturity. It is angry and fatherless, so it kills. This is the beast taking on a human form in the second generation: Adam's unclean, disobedient spirit is over his house and the nation.

The greedy, animalistic, and frustrated spirit is manifest in his son. This is when one brother kills another. It is the result of two sons not having an image from God over their lives. Their father and mother's lust destroyed the government of God. The serpent is taking on a human form. When the serpent of deception fully blossoms, it takes on the spirit of the lion. This is when the pride began and destruction becomes inevitable.

In the animal kingdom, the male lion drives his male sons away as early as three months old. The sons might get to stay until they are two years of age. The female lion, along with her daughters, remains and is forced to hunt for food. She teaches the baby female lions how to hunt and catch prey. When they bring it back, the male eats first.

The sons are forced out of the house without training. They will hunt until they find a female. It is in the nature of the young male lion to treat his female just like his father treated his mother. This young lion does not have to see or remember the abuse. It is in his nature to be just like his father. This is the spirit Adam released when he fell into lust. He released the serpent's nature.

Men and women will be unfaithful to each other after the lion spirit appears. They will have a violent, cruel nature. The government one day will become a place where women go for food stamps and a medical card in order to survive. Children will be left hungry, angry, and fatherless. The government will remain divided because men and women will live in lust and disorder. All of this is the nature of Satan. He is as a roaring lion. God expected His fatherhood to manifest in Adam. Adam was supposed to guard and protect his wife. Instead, he walked out of the presence of God. He became lustful and greedy. A woman must be corrected and loved. She needs protection and instructions. A man must never let a woman pull him away from God.

The Hebrew word for a young lion is *kephiyr* (kef-eer), which means "a village." It makes reference to the village having walls and a young lion covered with a mane. The *Strong's* reference number for the term *young lion* is 3715. The mane is the bushy fur around a male lion's head. The female does not have a mane. This is how you can tell them apart. Both are dangerous. The male is the beast that uses the lioness to get prey.

The spirit of the young lion entered government when the first family sinned. This is the beginning of the village. A village is a small group of houses knitted together. All Satan needed is the first house. One family in the village started a brand new government order. This would allow the serpent spirit to begin its municipality as the population increases. A municipality is a community combined into one governing body. It is organized as a legal corporation. The local affairs of the municipality are handled through their own system of belief. It can be a group of people ready to live life without God.

The world has become disordered and lustful. Governments ordered in the way that God would want are being destroyed. The human population is doing whatever it wants. The spirit of the young lion is present right now. In the Old Testament, we see the spirit of the lion manifested in Pharaoh.

Everything wicked in the Old Testament entered in as a result of the first family. Both Adam and Eve are a picture of one government. Their greed released the spirit of the young lion. The walls in the spirit realm went up immediately. God was locked out. He had no place to lay His head. This means that God does not have a male authority figure to operate through. In the spirit realm, the government has already been claimed by the beast. The spirit of the lion is now in authority. The only thing this spirit needs is a society that would build cities and towers that totally dishonor God. The animalistic behavior of the flesh would manifest. Humanity would soon see how destructive and cruel the flesh is without God.

In the beginning of the next two chapters, I will show

the beast in operation. This is when the flesh notices the beauty of a woman. The spirit of the woman is not considered or examined. Men began to marry whomever they want. God will not keep trying to take someone somewhere they continue to refuse to go.

> Whoso findeth a wife findeth a good thing, and obtaineth favor of the LORD.
> —PROVERBS 18:22

When a man does not have the mind of God, he does not know what to find. He will also operate in selfishness having more than one woman. None of the women will be good enough to marry as far as he is concerned. On the other hand, God is saying, "You do not have the right to look for a wife when I am still looking for you." It is impossible for a man to choose a wife when he rejects God. This is why he will eventually divorce the wife that he was not faithful to. Hold on. It works both ways. Many women have been unfaithful to a man who wanted nothing but the best for them and their family.

Keep in mind, I am also writing things out of the storms of my own life. My husband has always said there are two sides to every story. Sometimes we can care more about one side of the story than the other. I have written many books. They have been sitting for years, as far back as 1995. I have been sitting at home since the end of 2003. I have cried. I have suffered and served in my own house. In the presence of God, I have watched my dreams die. Right now I am looking at ashes. As God moves me closer to being released, I speak and write with the hands and mind of God.

As I look back over the years, I can think of many things that have been said about men, all of which may seem true in the sight of the many women who have been hurt. It does not matter if it was a girl who never knew her father. Maybe it was the one who was raped by him. Overall, every woman has her private definition of what a father is. Our first definition of a man was determined in our mind according to what kind of man was in the house. God is calling daughters to forgive their fathers. He wants to free you from the hurt that came because of who left or raped you.

Where forgiveness does not take place, you will see a woman giving herself away to several different men. If hopelessness steps in, she may burn in lust for another woman. If she does not know her own value, neither can she define love. She is left thirsting for something her father never gave her. This woman is bleeding because she is uncovered. Many women are broken because disorder and lust are on a rampage.

On the other hand, our sons have been left angry, hungry, and bitter. Their fathers were not present. Some of them were raped or abused by an uncle. They have been trained by the men who mistreated their mother. God wants us to understand how we have been our own worst enemy. The serpent spirit has taken on a human form.

When lust, greed, and deception get into the family,

the next generation feels the pain. This is the fruit of the first family's having been deceived by the serpent's lustful spirit. The anger and pain of lust are manifested in Cain. The judgment of lust is placed on Abel. One brother seeks to kill the other. God is locked out because man is in authority. God is a Spirit without a body to operate through. This is the beginning of the roaring lion. He is operating in the kingdom that God chose for Himself. He is using the family to attack each other and God.

Through my study, I have found that in the animal kingdom a lion roars when he is afraid. This animal has a savage, violent, cruel nature. The roar of the lion manifested when Cain killed Abel. Cain was angry, afraid, inexperienced, and unable to please God. It was up to his father, Adam, to tell him what type of offering God wanted. Cain is like a son who does not have a father; or, if he does, he is backslidden. Cain represents the men who came to God but were not able to surrender completely to the Father's will. He also represents the men who have killed their brothers. Cain is the individual who attacks those who pleased God. He is the man who has done wrong and then runs instead of receiving correction.

All of this is the spirit of the lion. This is exactly what is happening today. Many men are angry, hurt, and tired of trying. Nobody trained them, so they have been left to figure things out on their own. This has produced in them pride, arrogance, and a lack of trust for other people. When they needed someone, nobody was there. Now they are adults, and they are afraid to trust.

It is hard for some men to communicate. They think long and meditate hard. They are heavy on thinking and very introverted when it comes to expressing themselves. A man becomes used to himself, and he has never been nurtured. Nobody has ever built him up, so he tears everyone down. These men really want love. It is hard to have a relationship with men like him. He often uses women yet never intended to hurt them. The spirit of lust is in his genes. It is the curse of iniquity that came on them from the womb. God only knows what kind of spirit was pounding the womb of their mother when the child was waiting to be born.

Lust and greed within parents has left daughters vulnerable to being mistreated. Young sons often disrespect and use girls because they were not trained by their fathers. Women have seduced men with their bodies. Some men willingly help women who are in need of money by letting them trade it in exchange for sex. This is the spirit of the lion, because the spirit of the lion is also connected to the spirit of prostitution. God forbade a woman to sell her body to put bread on the table. God help the man who has abused his wife, refused to give her money, but then gives his money for sex from other women who are helpless. God is not pleased. This is the nature of the beast.

In the Last Days, water will cover the earth. It is the first sign of the beast marking his territory. In the animal kingdom, a beast marks his territory by urinating on it. This tells other beasts that the territory is taken. This raises several questions. I will also give you a riddle. I will not answer the questions. Neither will I answer the riddle. I will leave clues throughout this book. Here it is; it will be a preview of my next book:

> What does it mean to sow to your flesh? What does it mean to reap corruption?

Today you have learned much about the lion. In conclusion we can call it the spirit of prostitution. When a man and woman fall into lust, nobody wins except the lion spirit. It has a share, while the two parties run off into lust. What is the lion's share?

For years, Satan has been establishing new territories. He is destroying nations because of lust and greed. The ultimate goal is to leave mankind fighting each other. This spirit does not care who dies. His only desire is to have a female that he can use. God's divine order will be set in the nations when the female surrenders to God. This raises one question: Who is this female that the lion is using?

On the first day of Creation, God created heaven and the earth. At this time, the waters were still. On the second day of Creation, God separated the waters from the waters. He also put a firmament in the midst of the waters. This raises three questions: What happens when the firmament breaks? Why is water covering the nation? Who controls the flow of the waters? It also begs yet more questions: Who is the root out of the dry ground? What is the root of all evil?

As I close out this chapter, I will give you a riddle. They are no longer one bone, but two. The bones have been broken and chewed up.

May I give you another clue?

The bones were seen by Ezekiel. They were scattered all over the ground. Who or what is eating the bones up? What is going on in the ground? At last, I see a woman. This woman is holding a branch. She is using it to beat her children. God wants her to give Him the branch. This branch has become her weapon. The branch makes everyone cry. It is a deadly weapon. The branch caused Adam to die. Who in the world is this woman? How did she get this branch? Can this woman be delivered? Who does the branch represent?

This is the pattern of the skeptic. He is the scorpion in a rage. His tail is in the stinging position. (The scorpion has a grave.) This is the spirit of Jezebel. I will bring the Old Testament with the New. I will show you Jezebel's death. This woman is still not through. Her spirit remains forever. She has come back for the ground. She has caused so many deaths. (Her spirit rules the water now.) Yet, the scorpion continually stings. Death is singing a song. Where is the scorpion's grave? Where did Adam go wrong?

Chapter 2

# THE PUDENDA AND THE HEART

THE *PUDENDA* IS another word for the genitals. I will give you the Hebrew word for flesh. It will include the word *pudenda*. Adam said that the woman is flesh of his flesh and bone of his bones. I will give you all of the comparisons in the beginning of the next chapter. Adam's lifestyle will determine the outcome of God's messengers who will be born into the earth. His lifestyle will determine what kind of news and doctrines will be spread throughout the world.

Adam and Eve are the beginning of God's government and all human life. God expected Adam to cover his wife. She is the beginning of the church. He is the priest that would cover what comes out of him. Both of them have God's spirit. Together they would cover the ground. The ground is a picture of the first womb. The ground is the place of their beginning. Adam is the face of God. The face of God is seen on the first day of Creation. The face of God is called out of the ground on the sixth day of Creation. The face of God would cover the entire earth.

This becomes a picture of men who would have the image of God. Adam's lifestyle will determine what kind of spirit the next generation will have. Lust and greed for the forbidden fruit becomes a picture of a man who is selfish and greedy. This will be the beginning of God striving with men.

In Genesis 6:3 God said, "My spirit shall not always strive with man, for that he also is flesh: yet his days shall be an hundred and twenty years." The Hebrew word for flesh is *basar* (baw-sawr). It means flesh, and includes the entire body of a person. It also makes reference to the pudenda, which is the sex organ of the male. This word also means nakedness and skin. The *Strong's* reference number for the word *flesh* is 1320. The word *basar* (baw-sawr) comes from the Hebrew word *basar* (baw-sar). It refers to something that is fresh or full and rosy, such as being cheerful. It also suggests something that is a messenger that preaches, publishes, or delivers good tidings. The *Strong's* reference number for *basar* is 1319.

In Genesis 6:1–2, the human population began to increase on the earth very quickly. During this time, the sons of God saw how attractive the women were. As time progressed, the men chose wives. According to Scripture, they married any women they wanted. God then made the declaration that His Spirit would not always strive with men.

Mankind was put here to be a messenger for God. His

## The Pudenda and the Heart

plan was for them to preach the good news, which is the gospel.

Adam had already fallen. His belly became his God. This opened the door for the beast to bring in everything God forbade. The earthly house that God once dwelled in was then occupied by the serpent spirit.

Satan then began to manifest his works. He would use creation to do his dirty work. They were undisciplined, selfish, and lustful. They were producing children after their own flesh. The DNA of man was now contaminated. God's Spirit was no longer in humanity. Eating the forbidden fruit released the serpent spirit.

This was the second time God was robbed. The first robbery was when God lost Adam. Now, the lust continued and God would lose generations to come. The curse entered the belly, or womb, of the woman. Adam became a partaker when he could have been used to correct her. Greed caused both of them to lose the battle. This greed is the first manifestation of Jezebel. When two people disrespect God, they eventually will disrespect each other.

Satan is the devourer. He is also the seedeater. He used Adam and Eve to eat the fruit that God forbade. This would give an opportunity to attack their bellies. In the natural world, it looked like they ate from a tree. In the spirit realm, they became one with another spirit. They proved to be selfish, lustful, and greedy. Their spoken words would no longer have power. Greed for

God's portion pulled them out of rank, causing women eventually to become strong weapons against men. Adam was left powerless. Lust for God's portion would produce a root to all evil. Jezebel had not been born. Her spirit was already at work in Eve. Many men would be destroyed by the Jezebel spirit, which takes any opportunity to kill everything that passes through the womb.

Deception would rule this woman. The serpent spirit in her would shut the mouth of the prophets. Jezebel's spirit will run free. This is what happens when disorder enters the home. A no-name society will be born. They will hate God and totally disrespect human lives and God.

Jezebel is a woman who was eaten by the dogs. In the natural, the dogs devoured her. In the spirit realm, it is a manifestation of what happens to a woman when a man supports her disorder. Once again, everything goes back to the forbidden fruit. The first woman became selfishly deceived and greedy. Many of the wicked things that happened to men in the Bible came as a result of disorderly women. Once again I say to the men, stand up! Speak up! Find out what the forbidden fruit is. Then, afterward, stand with your wife and the two of you must help each other.

Another manifestation of Jezebel is seen in Pharaoh. He is hardhearted and greedy. His mission is to use women to destroy male babies. It is a picture of a man who is abusive with his authority and dishonorable toward women. He has no respect for the womb or what comes from it. Pharaoh's desire is to destroy the male babies. This is the serpent spirit at work. It does not respect anything that can reproduce. It chooses to devour it. This is also the spirit of the lion, which drives his sons away, as I stated earlier.

In the Last Days, the serpent and the lion spirits will fully manifest. This is when a woman will willingly kill her babies legally through abortion. She will take on the mind of a dragon. It is a picture of a woman who has been attacked by the serpent spirit that is manifested in many men. Men like those would choose to get a woman pregnant and then leave. Marriage and family are considered dishonorable, and not an honor. This is a picture of a broken government.

All of these things will lead to prostitution. Women will be forced to sleep around for money. Men will use a woman and think nothing of it, and that woman will end up having five children by three different men. And some of those men likely already had a wife and children. But that would not stop them from chasing another woman. This is lust, greed, disorder, and a serpent spirit in the house.

The first family divided the kingdom. In the Last Days, many people will have relationships with Christ. We will see great ministries shattered. God needs just one man who understands what the forbidden fruit means to Him. This man will call for a global repentance. God has chosen this man. This raises two questions: Why does divorce continue? What type of religious spirits would come as a result of the first family? When a person eats the forbidden fruit, the serpent spirit will drive the two spouses eventually to walk away from each other because one or both of them wants something God forbids. The religious spirit is the spirit that entered in when the first family sinned. This religious spirit still lives in many couples. They want a spouse, but they do not want God. Others just want sex but do not want God or a marriage.

In Mark 10:1–5, Jesus had just come into the coast of Judaea. The Pharisees came before Him with a question. They asked if it was lawful for a man to put away his wife. They did this to tempt Him. Jesus asked, "What did Moses command you [to do]?" (Mark 10:3). They responded that Moses suffered men to write a bill of divorcement, and put her away. Jesus answered saying Moses wrote the precept because of the hardness of heart of people like these Pharisees.

The Greek word for hardness and heart is *sklerokardia* (sklay-rok-ar-dee-ah). It is feminine and of a compound of the words *skleros* (sklay-ros) 4642 and *kardia* (kar-dee-ah) 2588; it means hardheartedness, which deals with being destitute of spiritual perception. The *Strong's* reference number for hardness of heart is 4641. Many are destitute of spiritual perception. They have no knowledge of God. Some have very little knowledge. There are others who know it all. These men were very religious. They had no respect for God. This is a serpent spirit. He refuses to change so he tempts God.

## The Pudenda and the Heart

The term *destitute* refers to lack. It usually means not having what you need. These men were in a debate. Let's look at the word *perception*. This is the ability to perceive. How can a man run a house when he is blind? Jesus knew these men could not see. Jesus would not release them to divorce. You see, Jesus is their key. These men did not want deliverance. They just wanted to be free. Their hearts were very hard. Like a beast, they were cold and dry. They had no relationship with Christ. This made it easy to tell their wives good-bye. The Greek word *sklerokardia* (sklay-rok-ar-dee-ah) is feminine and a compound of the Greek word *skleros* (sklay-ros), which refers to being dry, hard, tough, harsh, and fierce. The *Strong's* reference number for the word *skleros* (sklay-ros) is 4642.

Jesus said their hearts were hard. Take notice that they were hard and dry. Did you notice their hearts are tough, too? It even means harsh. Look at the word *fierce*, which means "violent and cruel." This spirit goes back to Adam. Greed has made men religious and brutal.

Jesus knew their very thoughts. He knew their feelings and their minds. These men were brokenhearted. I do not mean hurt by their wives, but brokenhearted in their spirits. Their hearts (spirits) were hard and dry. They had no relationship with God. This would make it easy to tell any woman good-bye.

This spirit goes back to Adam. The serpent spirit is working overtime. Lust and greed have produced divorce. Now men are religious and blind. They are right in the midst of the Savior. You would think they would break down and change. In the Last Days, religion will increase, yet the family will hate the name of the Son of God.

Eating the forbidden fruit opened the door to every kind of curse. This includes religious spirits and denominations of all kinds. Man was separated from God. He was subject to become divorced because of it. His heart became hard because of greed. This is the beginning of much division.

Next I will talk about the Pharisees. They were religious. These men did not know or respect Christ. This spirit is present in people today. The Pharisees refused to be corrected. The only thing they are interested in is making themselves happy. Their definition for happiness is coming to church and complaining about someone they do not want anymore. The Bible never named what the problem might have been with their wives. Nevertheless, you will see that these men were not in their place.

God will always deal hard with the man. He holds them responsible. In the beginning, God created the woman out of the man. She received her image from the man. The man was supposed to continue with the process God completed. God expected him to teach and instruct her concerning the things of God. Adam failed to correct his wife. He went along with her disorder, and that disorder caused division, divorce, hard-heartedness, lust, greed, and religion.

## The Pudenda and the Heart

It was the same spirit that operated in Pharaoh. It is a spirit that disrespects God's daughters and any type of governmental order that is consistent with the Word. The root of this spirit comes from Adam's wife. His agreement with the woman was a direct attack and dishonor toward God. Here is the scripture again. The Greek word for Pharisee will follow the scripture.

In Mark 10:1–5, Jesus had just come into the coast of Judaea. The Pharisees came before Him with a question. They asked if it was lawful for a man to put away his wife. This they did in order to tempt Him. Yet, Jesus asked them what Moses commanded them to do. They responded that Moses suffered to write a bill of divorcement, to put her away. Jesus answered saying Moses wrote that precept because of the hardness of their hearts.

The Greek word for Pharisees is *pharisaios* (far-is-ah-yos). This word is of the Hebrew origin and makes reference to one that is a separatist. The person is also exclusively religious. The *Strong's* reference number for the word *Pharisees* is 5330.

A separatist is one that withdraws. Separatists want to be on their own. At one time, they were a part of a larger group. They left with a heart like stone. These persons advocate their own religious beliefs. They have no sound guidelines at all. They advocate their own racial and political beliefs, all of which may be contrary to God's will.

This confusion is the work of the serpent. This means

God is not in the house. What is the nature of a serpent? How does a serpent run his house? The serpent does not raise its children. They give birth and leave them crawling. The babies come out eating whatever they see—and this is the same nature Adam released on us. This is why people use people. Men and woman have used each other. Everyone has had it hard, but now it is time to help one another.

God's apostolic government is still broken. He wants women to be protected by men. Remember, God is a spirit. This means that God is depending on the men. Many women are attacking men; to them, the man is just a dog. May I ask what spirit it is that has formed our men? The first woman let in this, but the "dog" is like a spirit. It entered in through Adam and Eve. This is the beginning of prostitution. The ground will eventually bleed.

The ground is the first womb. Out of it came a man. The man is a picture of the ground. God wanted the ground to reproduce. Another image is in the ground. This is the woman being brought out of the man. There were no graveyards around. How did the graveyard come about? How did death get in the plan? For now, let's talk about man. Adam is flesh of the woman's flesh. He is bone of the woman's bones. They ate the forbidden fruit, which represents the beginning of a no-name society in which the men and women despise each other and God.

Genesis 2:21–23 tells us, "God caused a deep sleep to

## The Pudenda and the Heart

fall upon Adam and he slept: and he took one of His ribs, and closed up the flesh instead thereof; And the rib, which the LORD God had taken from man, made he a woman, and brought her unto the man. And Adam said, This is now bone of my bones, and flesh of my flesh: she shall be called Woman, because she was taken out of Man." God is the Creator of all mankind. He was the first to put His hands on their ribs. He is also the one who put flesh on their bones. Everything was lovely. Giving God what He asked for would keep them free from disease.

When sin entered, God asked for tithes and offerings. This is God's way of going after the heart of mankind. Men and women would continue in lust. Many would not realize that their money is not what God wanted from the beginning. Man has become the serpent that allows Babylon to rule. The selfishness of the flesh has caused men and women to run over each other. Now they despise giving from their financial blessings.

The spirit of divorce is attacking men and women. Many are comfortable sleeping around. This raises two questions. First, how much are you willing to give now? And second, is there a man out there anywhere who is willing to say, "Teach me how to love You"? If there is such a man, God wants him to call a global repentance for all men. It is time to meet with the Holy Spirit.

In the presence of God, we will weep and cry out to Him. This is the time when God is turning the hearts of the fathers back to the sons. Everything that is dead shall live again in Him.

Eating the forbidden fruit released every act of sin. The first family released a serpent spirit into the atmosphere. Rape, murder, and the spirit of incest were waiting to manifest. The only thing these spirits needed was more bodies to operate through.

The dog is an actual animal, and it ate Jezebel. In the natural realm, it is a dog. In the spirit realm, it is a sign of what would manifest in the Last Days. Jezebel died, but her spirit remains. The Book of Revelation talks about her.

Today we have a no-name society and it despises God and has no respect for human life. The city that came out of the first family continues to this day because we do not know what seed God wants.

Let's look back at an Old Testament scripture. I want you to see what kind of heart is beating in the human race. It will also allow you to see how your spirit is shaped according to your obedience to God. When God asks you for something that you will not give Him, it will eventually produce a Pharaoh spirit in your house and, ultimately, over the nations. Genesis 6:5 says, "GOD saw that the wickedness of man was great in the earth, and that every imagination of the thoughts of his heart was only evil continually." In the next verse, it says, "It repented the LORD that he had made man on the earth, and it grieved him at his heart."

Take notice of these two Scripture verses. The word

*The Pudenda and the Heart*

*heart* is mentioned twice. The first time you see the word *heart*, it is talking about mankind. The second time talks about God's heart. In Exodus 4:21, it talks about Pharaoh's heart. The Hebrew definition for the heart of man, the heart of God, and the heart of Pharaoh are all the same.

As I give you the Hebrew definition for the word *heart*, it will reveal what kind of spirit entered the nation because of disobedience. Man became unclean because of his own lust. God created Adam in His image. The outcome of Adam's life established a pattern for everyone else. God needed Adam's body because God created the image for Himself. The forbidden fruit would determine the outcome of the family and the nations to come. Their image and heart would be deformed when the first man disobeyed. And as mentioned a few times earlier, the first family sinned.

This is the beginning of the lion spirit. It is a picture of a beast. Daniel gave a better description of it. He saw a lion. It stood up like a man. A human heart was given to it. The lion is the spirit of prostitution. This is the spirit that entered into mankind through the first family. Prostitution is driven by a deeper sin spirit than merely by a woman standing on a street corner. It is a spirit that lives in the world because we do not respect the womb or human lives.

The Hebrew word for heart is *Leb* (labe). The word *heart* used figuratively connotes feelings, the will, and even the intellect. It also can refer to the center of something. This word gives other descriptions of the heart such as to care, comfortable, consent, friendly, broken, hard, stiff, stout, doubled minded, and wise. The *Strong's* reference number for the word *heart* is 3820. The word *heart* is used very widely. It includes a person's feelings, their will, and their intellect or mind. Notice the definition for heart has several sub-definitions. The heart has the ability to be caring or to care for something. It can also be described by words such as *comfortable* and *consent*.

Adam's body is the earthly house God needed. He gave Adam dominion over all things. Adam would rule over the serpent. In the natural realm, it looked like an innocent animal that Adam was given authority over. In the spirit realm, it is a beastly spirit that needed a human body so that it could operate at its fullest.

Adam has the mind of God. He would care like God. He would also care for God. Adam has a human body with his Father's Holy Spirit. God wanted Adam to live in comfort and to be comfortable. With the mind of God, Adam would give consent or approval to the things God allows.

As we look at the definition for the word *heart*, we understand that the heart has the potential to be courageous and friendly. At the same time, it can be broken or become hard. The heart can be kind and wise. It can also be stiff, stout, and double-minded.

Adam's sins brought all mankind into successive ages of Pharaohs, each infected more deeply by sin. Men and women would have double minds. They would have the

## The Pudenda and the Heart

ability to be loving and caring. In the same moment, they can become hard and cruel. Nobody will understand that eating the forbidden fruit breaks the spirit or the heart of the individual. It produces a cruel, animalistic nature. Adam does not have a life without God. It becomes a picture of a man without a Father.

Adam's lifestyle would determine the outcome of the kingdom that God wanted. God helps the kingdom that is on the rise. The flesh will be cruel when it comes to children. The serpent will prevail when it comes to marriage. Sex with anyone will be considered acceptable. The world will set up prisons for those who are out of control. Mental institutions will be established for those who have gone insane. Starvation will be spread worldwide. Everything that God forbids will become legal. This is what we can expect when a man fails to name a woman and tell her what her assignment in God is, as Adam did in the Garden.

In the Last Days, there will be many women with merchant ships. They will have plenty of money, but no husbands. Many will say, "I don't need a man," yet they will have a man in their bed every night. Many women equate needing a man with needing a man for money. They do not understand that a legal covenant with one man is designed to keep the serpent spirit away from you.

God gave Adam dominion over all things, but God did not tell Adam how cruel and wicked the serpent is. God is the Father who will keep His children from being cursed. Adam would look into the face of an assassin spirit. He would never be intimidated. Adam would never know how deadly that spirit is. His Father never wanted him to know what this spirit could do to a man. All Adam had to do was obey. Adam would have to submit without question. God told him he could not eat the forbidden fruit. Adam would never wrestle with his flesh. He would enjoy one wife and produce a family for God.

This is the favor man had. The Holy Spirit would cover him if he understood discipline in the garden. He would also release fatherhood in the kingdom that God wanted. Sons would have an example. Living for God would be a privilege. Hearing from God would never be confusing or difficult. The family would not have to question what God wanted. They would have fathers who would teach them what God expected of them.

Adam chose to eat the fruit. Adam's body was God's house. Eating the fruit drove the spirit of the father out of Adam's earthly body. God's Spirit was no longer in Adam's house. The presence of God would no longer be in the world. Women will get used and hurt. Men will be left in authority and fatherless. They will blame God and curse Him.

This is the beginning of the Pharaoh's rule. They will rule, abuse, and kill everything that comes out of the womb. The next scripture I quote will reveal how divided was the kingdom that God wanted. Women were left praying. They were midwives. These women were used to assist other women who were having babies. Pharaoh wanted all male babies dead. This is the spirit of the lion. It does not respect anything that can reproduce. It does not want to take care of what has been produced. It wants to use women to kill anything that represents male authority. The only thing this spirit wants is a city filled with women. It does not mind reproduction, as long as the male children are killed. What is this spirit really up to? What kind of spirit or people will be left if all the male babies are killed?

Read the entire first chapter of Exodus. Pharaoh ruled over those who loved God. He treated them like slaves. They were forced to build him treasure cities. He wanted to use the women to destroy the male babies. His plan was to have only women left. This is the lion spirit. God never wanted women left uncovered. God wanted women to be protected by men. The first woman was supposed to honor, respect, and help the man. God expected the family to be fruitful and multiply. After the first family ate the forbidden fruit, the woman did not know that she was disrespecting herself when she dishonored the man. Their greed and lust released the spirit of the dragon. This is when a bottomless pit is produced. When this happens, everything you wanted, worked for, and gave birth to will be completely destroyed or divided.

Having a hard heart is the result of being greedy. You cannot devour something that God wants for Himself. This is what Adam did. The same animalistic, disrespectful spirit is manifested in Pharaoh. Keep in mind it started with the first woman.

In Exodus 4:21, it says that God was going to harden Pharaoh's heart. This happens only because of the mindset Pharaoh had. God did not make him that way. This is the selfish, proud nature that entered in through Adam. He knew better and failed to correct his wife. He agreed with her, as I have already stated. Now, disobedience continues. It has become more progressive.

Pride is operating in another man. He refuses to hear God. He wants to use and misguide women who pray. It is a picture of a man in authority who is abusive. He does not want a wife, he just wants to use women. Most of all, in the Pharaoh example, this type of man desires to kill the babies because he does not have or pray to receive the heart of a father.

In the Last Days, women will be as the praying women in the days of Pharaoh. We will be assisting women who are giving birth. We will also be giving birth. This will be the hour when God is turning the hearts of women toward His face. The King of kings lives in you. His name is Jesus. He wants you to prepare a place for the man you are laying next to. This means you will fight for your husband until the Spirit of the King comes alive in him. It starts with cooking and cleaning up the house that both of you live in. This is where I am. My wisdom has come as a result of cleaning my own toilets and mopping my own floors. I have learned to smile while serving at home when I knew I would like to be somewhere preaching.

This is where we lost the battle in the beginning. The

first woman ran in front of the man. She became lustful and greedy. Ever since that day, it has been trouble in the house for the family.

God told me that there is a place in the atmosphere that has been unoccupied since Adam's Fall. Mankind does not know what seed God really wants. God revealed to me that the space was occupied when Prophetess Juanita Bynum did her book, *No More Sheets*. Her journey has been long. God wanted her to be covered by a man that could say, "Teach me how to love You." When she got married, it created a divine apostolic government. Together the two of them brought God out of the box.

This is the beginning of God looking for His face—mankind. This is the hour when God is looking at our relationships. Man is the face of God, but man is having sex with a lot of women. Man was created to be the face of God, but he is burning in lust and needs help. Man has not been taught to honor marriage. Man must become willing to say, "Teach me how to love You." I say to Bishop Weeks and Prophetess Juanita, God told me that both of you have fought a good fight. It was not easy.

Lust and greed destroyed God's image in the beginning. Everything in this hour is about man, the face of God. Man has been left angry and hungry. Man has been left homeless and fatherless. Man is on drugs and shooting drugs into his arms using needles. Man is drunk under a bridge. Man has a wife and three girlfriends. Man is behind bars.

Man has mastered and organized street gangs all over the world. Man has been left without training and skills for life. Man does not know his own father. Man has been abused. Man can no longer be seen in the ground.

We are in the End Times. Everything is going back to seedtime and harvest. We have entered paradise in the spirit realm. For years, God has asked for tithes and offerings. We had no idea that our money is not the seed God is really after. We have continued in lust, greed, and selfishness.

Once again, it is about to become dark. Two spirits will be moving. God is looking for His face. When He cannot find His face, the waters will rule. This raises one question: What does the water have to do with man?

Chapter 3

# TWO THIEVES AND A YARDSTICK

THE CHURCH HAS been in rebellion since Adam's Fall. The bones are very dry. The people of the church are without life. The worship is not pure. We have become as sounding brass. (See 1 Corinthians 13:1.) The heat has been turned up to provoke us to search our hearts. This will cause us to be moved with compassion. God will use us to reach all mankind. Whosoever will let Him, come!

In the next two Scripture passages I quote, I will refer to the Hebrew word for the word *flesh* that I discussed in chapter 2. Both scriptures will have the same definition. These words will reveal what God wanted from Adam. You will see the responsibility that one man has. He must cover, instruct, and name the woman. She is a picture of the government and the church. She must honor, respect, and help the man. Her choice will determine the outcome of the messengers that God wanted.

Genesis 2:21–25 says, "God caused a deep sleep to fall upon Adam and he slept: and he took one of his ribs, and closed up the flesh instead thereof; And the rib, which the LORD God had taken from man, made he a woman, and brought her unto the man. And Adam said, This is now bone of my bones, and flesh of my flesh: she shall be called Woman, because she was taken out of Man. Therefore shall a man leave his father and his mother, and shall cleave unto his wife: and they shall be one flesh. And they were both naked, the man and his wife, and were not ashamed." God is the Father. His Spirit is at work in one body. Several things are taking place. Let me show you the fullness of everything that is happening in this verse. A woman is receiving life. She is being shaped by the Holy Spirit. Her image comes from the man that is in her life. The man in her life has been shaped by his Father. The two of them are one body. Both of them have the Father's Spirit.

Adam said, "We are one person. Your body is mine. We have the same skin. My sex organ (pudenda) is yours. We will produce the same kind. We will preach the same message. We will carry the good news. Many messengers will come out of us. This is the will of the Lord for our house."

Let's look at the same scripture again. I will show you something else that was taking place. I will also tell you what Adam meant when he said she is "bone of my bones." God's Spirit is moving. The Father is releasing His son to be loved. The son has the Spirit of his Father. Greatness is in the son. The Father pulls it out of him. The son is prepared and groomed for ministry. It is revealed to him by his Father. The ministry is a woman. She is a picture of the church. The son must instruct and cover her. He is responsible for her destiny. She must be led by the man. He must name this woman. She must listen to the man. They cannot fail to communicate. If they miss God's timing, the Babylon spirit will cause her to dishonor him and God.

As they prepare to be fruitful and multiply, both must beware that the choices they make will determine the kind of spirit their children will have. Their choices will affect the kingdom that God wants to come on the earth. God told Adam and Eve to be fruitful and multiply. God expected them to produce more messengers. The messengers will have the same spirit that God gave Adam. The image will change if the two of them become selfish and greedy. Lust would cause man to strive against God's Spirit. Correcting men with a selfish nature would be a lifelong battle.

In Genesis 6:1–2, the human population had begun to increase. During this time, the sons of God saw how attractive the women were. As time progressed, the men chose wives. According to Scripture, they married any women they wanted. The next verse, Genesis 6:3, says, "The LORD said, My spirit shall not always strive with man, for that he also is flesh: yet his days shall be an hundred and twenty years."

In this passage, God says, "My spirit shall not always strive with man." The word *strive* refers to an attempt or trying very hard. It also means "to struggle with, fight for or contend with."

Have you ever been in a battle with your son or sons?

Have you often wondered why the warfare was intense? This is what disorder and lust did to the human population. It left Father God in a conflict with humanity. It also means mankind will be in a conflict with each other. The serpent spirit will use mankind to wound, afflict, and kill one another. This is from the sixth chapter of the Book of Genesis. Cain has already killed Abel. Notice what the Father said, "My spirit shall not always strive with man, for that he is also flesh" (Gen. 6:3). God is saying that He will not continue to fight with man's flesh. He will not continue to struggle with man when man is supposed to be His messengers. God is also saying that the Holy Spirit will not keep contending with man about his pudenda. God says, "I am Father God, but I have been locked out of your lives and your earthly bodies."

This is what happens when greed and lust come in. The first family caused this disorder. This spirit still exists today. Many men marry whomever they want. God is striving with men. Nobody wants to stand corrections. God cannot get one dime out of your dollar. Now men marry and sleep with any woman they want. Humanity has become even more selfish, lustful, and greedy.

This does not stop God's love for humanity. Men and women must love like God. Yet, how can this be possible when someone gets our women pregnant but then leaves them hungry? She is then forced to struggle just to make ends meet. The sins of men have been swept under the rug under a conclusion that says that even though the man loves God, he is just struggling, and this is why he behaves as he does.

Both men and women have been left fatherless and hungry. God expected every home to have a father and mother who are legally married to each other. Children will be born and left crawling. The home will have a mother and a boyfriend. He may or may not be the biological father of the children. In these Last Days, it just gets worse and worse.

Many women will take on the dragon's mentality. Children will be left for the bottomless pit. The father and the mother will be nowhere to be found.

God is a Spirit. His Spirit needs an image. His Spirit is depending on your body to cover your children. Let's look at what Adam meant when he said the woman is "bone of my bones."

The Hebrew word for bone is *etsem* (eh'-tsem), It says the bone is strong and an extension of the body. The word *substance* is used figuratively, which shows us how necessary the bones are in order for the flesh to have its shape. The *Strong's* reference number for bone and bones is 6106.

This word comes from the Hebrew word *atsam*, (aw'-tsam). It means to bind fast, which means to close (the eyes). It also means to be or make powerful or numerous. To crunch or break the bones is also in this definition. The *Strong's* reference number is 6105.

Adam knew Eve came from him. He acknowledged their oneness. He declared that they had the selfsame body. Their bones were connected one to the other. Both of them had the same strength. They had strong substance and faith. There was no division between them.

Adam knew his decision would "crunch" (this term is used in the Strong's definition for *atsam*) both their bones. Disobedience would bind them. Their eyes would be closed. Adam's mind would be blinded. He would not be able to defeat the serpent. His spoken words would be powerless.

This is why in the New Testament it says the peoples' minds are blinded. Greed and lust have disrupted the plan of God. Eating the forbidden fruit leaves a man feeling hopeless and blind. It also causes continual warfare in the mind of people who are born again today.

The serpent spirit causes you to view your circumstances in a hopeless manner. Many people pray and do not see results. On many occasions, God rebukes the devourer when a person gives. He did it because your money is a seed; however, your money is not the seed God is really after. He used it to draw you back to Him.

Many men and women will not give. Some sleep with whomever they want. They have cursed the church with their mouth and call us greedy. They fail to understand that we all have sinned and must repent from our sins. When we repent, God positions the church to speak into the lives of people. God allowed us to become the parents for children that were left. We are speaking into the destiny of men and women who never knew their parents. They are devastated and hopeless because they have been left with their umbilical cord uncut. This means they have been cursed by their parents and the sins the parents committed. It is the church that will minister deliverance to them. God does not want them to hate their parents and then turn out just like them.

The Hebrew word for bones that I discussed earlier is the same one as the term used in Ezekiel 37:1–11. In the third verse, God asked, "Can these bones live?" The people of God were cold, dead, and dry. The beast had swallowed them up. This is the spirit that entered in because of Adam's disobedience. Mankind became hard-hearted and religious because of greed. Let's look at the same scripture once more. I want to show you something else that God wanted to establish in the beginning.

As we've already seen, Genesis 2:21–25 describes how God created Eve from Adam. God wanted another house. Adam's body belongs to God. That body has a spouse. Look at God's Spirit. It is moving in the man. Adam must only surrender. This is his Father's plan. What is taking place? Multiplication is on the rise. Reproduction will continue. Adam must abide.

Did you notice in that scripture verse, that the man must cleave to his wife? God said, "Leave your mother and father." Adam needs his wife. Take notice again. God is doing something in the land. He put the first man and woman here. This is the beginning of parenthood in the land.

As you know, they ate the fruit. This is the beginning

of the lion's den. The human flesh can be horrible. It has no respect for God. He expected man to take dominion. He wanted man to be His rod. This raises a question: How do you know for sure that Adam is God's rod? I will answer this question now.

Let's go back to the forth day of the Creation. God devised a plan before He spoke to the ground. His will is done in heaven. God is ready to make a sound. His kingdom is ready to come. God would start with a man. God was thinking about Adam before He created him. Let me show you God's kingdom plan. In Genesis 1:16, it says, "And God made two great lights; the greater light to rule the day, and the lesser light to rule the night: he made the stars also." Keep in mind, this is the fourth day.

The Hebrew word for stars is *kowkab* (ko-kawb). It is defined as a star. The word *prince* is in the definition and is used figuratively. The *Strong's* reference number for the word *stars* is 3556.

A prince is defined as "a male monarch." He is the single or sole ruler of a state. His rank of rule is below that of a king. God is setting up His heavenly estate. He placed a pattern in the sky. God did not have to debate. The stars represent men of authority. They would cover the land and protect woman by faith.

In Genesis 1:26–28, God said, "Let us make man in our image, after our likeness: and let them have dominion over the fish of the sea, and over the fowl of the air, and over the cattle, and over all the earth, and over every creeping thing that creepeth upon the earth. So God created man in his own image, in the image of God created he him; male and female created he them. And God blessed them, and God said unto them, Be fruitful, and multiply, and replenish the earth, and subdue it: and have dominion over the fish of the sea, and over the fowl of the air, and over every living thing that moveth upon the earth." This was the sixth day of Creation. God spoke these words over the land. He was speaking to the stars. The man would be God's prince in the land. The first man was God's gate. Let me show you how God operates.

God already knew the man needed a helpmate. God operates in faith. Notice how He spoke in the land. He spoke of these things in their finished state. God created them male and female. Did you notice God already had blessed them? Then, He would reveal His plan. God would speak to the ground. The ground released the first prince in the land.

This prince is God's scepter. He would keep God's order in the land. A scepter is a rod. It is often seen in a king's hand. Adam is God's scepter. Together they will protect the land. Adam must continually submit to God's process. If he fails, a lion spirit can enter in. This raises three questions: Who did God show the stars to after Adam failed fatherhood? Why did a star appear when Jesus was born? And, what are the stars doing now?

Now, let's go back to Genesis 2:21–25 one more time. God produced Eve out of Adam. He used one of Adam's ribs. God closed up the flesh instead. This means the devourer could not destroy them. He could not destroy what would pass through their womb. God was obligated to them as long as they obeyed Him concerning the forbidden fruit. After they ate the fruit, the door for the princes that God wanted to be born was closed.

In the spirit realm, the serpent spirit claimed them. Men would be born with hearts like stone. Nobody would understand that lust and greed destroyed what God planned for every man.

In the Last Days, it will become dark again. The spirit of men will dominate the atmosphere. Although they live in the earth, their spirits will create strong winds and dangerous storms. As hurricanes come and go, they will have male and female names. This raises two questions: Who is Hurricane Andrew? Who is Hurricane Katrina?

In Daniel 7:5, it talks about three ribs. They were in the mouth of a bear. The ribs were between the bear's teeth. He was told to arise and devour much flesh. I looked up the Hebrew word for Adam and Eve's ribs. They have the same definition as the word is used in Daniel 7:5.

Greed put our ribs and bones in the mouth of the devourer. It separated the first family from God. Our hearts would become hard and religious. This attack would affect the government as we see it today. Men would debate over things God forbids. The beast—again, Satan working against mankind—would cause them to condone it. This is the result of being lustful and greedy.

Adam and Eve were the first thieves. This reminds me of the two thieves on the cross. They were in the midst of the Anointed One. He sacrificed for them to have all. Selfishness caused one to want paradise without denying the flesh. Nobody will win when you are in love with your flesh. This means you cannot be first. One must think of others. Most of all, you cannot devour something God has already asked you to give unto Him.

The two thieves also remind me of husbands and wives. Both of them are in the midst of the anointing. They have their cross and claim to know Jesus, but one or both are saying, "I don't have to take this." You cannot win if you decide that it is only about you. Once again, it will not be easy. You must learn to consider each other. Both of you must walk by faith and not by what you see. Walking by faith does not mean remaining selfish while the other person tolerates it. This raises two questions: Who is Dagon? And, who is Jezebel? I will show you the power of one woman's hands. It will reveal how these spirits, Dagon and Jezebel, entered in.

Eve's greed destroyed her house. She used her hands to tear it down. Adam agreed with it. He failed to bring correction. This is the spirit of Dagon and Jezebel. Dagon is the fish god. I will show you the comparisons. It is also the beginning of the mystery of Babylon. I will not discuss Babylon at this time. Men would eventually build an idol to worship. This would be their god.

They would also have a woman who is cruel and greatly deceived. This is the spirit of Jezebel. The end result is a society that kills one another and a court system that totally dishonors God.

In 1 Samuel 5:1–3, the philistines took the ark of God. They brought the ark into the house of Dagon. The ark was placed next to Dagon. The next day, Dagon had fallen with his face to the ground. This carved image lay in front of the ark. The presence of God in the ark knocked Dagon down. The people sat Dagon up again.

The presence of God once lived in man. His Spirit does not have an image. God lost His face in the garden. Man is the face of God. Many men are angry and fatherless. They are princes and do not even know it. In the Last Days, God will use one man and woman to get the ark. This will be the beginning of the turning of the world. Without a doubt, God will visit every house. This will also be the beginning of a great shaking.

In 1 Samuel 5:4, Dagon had fallen upon his face again in front of the ark. His head and both the palms of his hands were cut off upon the threshold. Only the stump of Dagon was left. The presence of God in the ark destroyed the Philistines' idol.

Dagon was an idol that had no power. The Philistines worshiped this carved image they made. This is idol worship in the presence of God. The presence of God in the ark destroyed the Philistines' idol. This should have been the end of that spirit. The people used their hands to stand it right back up. Satan prevailed because

*Two Thieves and a Yardstick*

mankind is disobedient. The devil is still using hands just like he did Eve's.

The presence of God in the ark was being abused. This is a picture of Eve showing dishonor toward Adam. The woman dishonored her husband completely. Eating the forbidden fruit put the next generations in idol worship. Nothing has changed, even up to today. Men will sit in God's presence and refuse to change. Women are guilty, too. The family has hurt each other.

Those who worship idols are happy. The family has insulted God. Everyone in the whole world is guilty. This raises three questions: What happens to a woman when her husband agrees with her disorder? What happens to a woman when her husband fails to correct her? What happens to a woman when she fails to take the warning God sends? I will answer these questions now. It will reveal God's judgment on a woman when she is never corrected.

In 2 Kings 9:1–10, Elisha the prophet called one of the children of the prophets. He gave him some oil and told him to anoint Jehu. God was going to destroy the house of Ahab. His wife was wicked. Her name was Jezebel. Satan used her to kill many servants who were God prophets. God declared that the dogs would eat Jezebel in the portion of Jezreel, and there would be none to bury her. Second Kings 9:30 says that when Jezebel herd Jehu was coming, "She painted her face, and tired her head, and looked out at a window." One might say she

55

## Mark of the Beast

put on some make up, fixed her hair, and then sat at the window.

> And as Jehu entered in at the gate, she said, Had Zimri peace, who slew his master? And he lifted up his face to the window, and said, Who is on my side? who? And there looked out to him two or three eunuchs. And he said, Throw her down. So they threw her down: and some of her blood was sprinkled on the wall, and on the horses: and he trode her under foot. And when he was come in, he did eat and drink, and said, Go, see now this cursed woman, and bury her: for she is a king's daughter. And they went to bury her: but they found no more of her than the skull, and the feet, and the palms of her hands. Wherefore they came again, and told him. And he said, This is the word of the Lord, which he spake by his servant Elijah the Tishbite, saying, In the portion of Jezreel shall dogs eat the flesh of Jezebel: And the carcase of Jezebel shall be as dung upon the face of the field in the portion of Jezreel; so that they shall not say, This is Jezebel.
> —2 Kings 9:31–37

This is the consequence of being manipulative, cunning, and hardhearted. Nobody is safe outside of God. You will not attack or shut off His peoples' voices. He will withdraw His hands from you—the devil is just waiting to destroy you. This is actually self-destruction. Rebellion will always leave a nation and any person uncovered.

Jezebel's spirit exists today. Men cannot be in authority the way God requires. They are being controlled by their wives. Some men have a controlling spirit like Jezebel. They are manipulative, cunning, hardhearted, and abusive. This is a force that will use anyone.

God has sent His anointing to deal with all evil. Man has been forgiven and restored. Mankind must confess Christ and receive Him as Lord. The Word of God will show you what God requires. Jesus is the example God uses to show a man how to submit to the Father. God wants this anointing, Christ, to live in every human being. This will empower everyone to be a weapon for God. They would speak the Word. It would produce a great harvest. Satan would have no one to use. This is what God wanted from Adam in the beginning.

Mankind has a will. God has told them to choose life. They have chosen to be thieves and robbers. They have refused to surrender their will. Some are rebuking demons, yet their prayers have not been answered. God will rebuke the devourer. He will do that by showing mankind what the forbidden fruit means to Him.

Let's go back into a couple of Scripture passages I discussed. I will compare both of them. Dagon was a carved image. Jezebel was a human being. Both of them have the same hands and palms. I will also give you the Hebrew word for Jezebel's feet. Eating the forbidden fruit produced idol worship and the fullness of Jezebel.

This is what happens when someone becomes selfishly deceived. Here is what continues when men do not correct it. First Samuel 5:4 says, "When they arose early on the morrow morning, behold, Dagon was fallen upon his face to the ground before the ark of the LORD; and the head of Dagon and both the palms of his hands were cut off upon the threshold; only the stump of Dagon was left to him." Second Kings 9:35 says, "They went to bury her [Jezebel]: but they found no more of her than the skull, and the feet, and the palms of her hands."

The Hebrew words for Dagon and Jezebel palms are the same. The Hebrew word is *kaph* (kaf). This word makes reference to the hollow center of the hand and its palms. The word *sole* is mentioned, which refers to the bottom surface of the foot. The word *power* is used figuratively in this definition. The Strong's reference number for palms is 3709.

This Hebrew word comes from the word *kaphaph* (kaw-faf), a primitive root that means to curve or bow down. The Strong's reference number for kaphaph is 3721.

The palm of your hands represents power. It also includes the sole and the foot. God is a spirit. He needed the first family to set his order in the globe. Their obedience would produce a society that respects one another. Instead they allowed greed to set another course.

The serpent is a creature that Adam was given dominion over. The serpent is a beast that wanted to express its true nature. It needed two human bodies to do so. This would bring him into the power of agreement with man. It will also declare that the first family has disagreed with God.

Adam is given power to tread on the serpent. Greed and lust will cause men and women to walk over each other. The beast that he once treaded on would eventually show how cruel it is. This Babylonian spirit will use men and women to destroy each other. Men and women will continually get married and remarried. They would not know that eating the forbidden fruit would cause two people to dishonor each other.

Dagon did not have a mind. Jezebel did. Men continued to rebel. This spirit now takes on a human form. The Philistines were declaring Satan as lord. They gave their life to idol worship. Satan was waiting to move in to kill men. All he needed was a woman to do it.

The Hebrew word for Dagon's and Jezebels' hands is the same. I want to give you some of the things that were written. You will see what is affected when your hands are not clean. You must give up being manipulative. You must stop your idol worship.

The Hebrew word for hands is *yad* (yawd), and makes reference to the hand being open. It indicates that the hands show power and direction for one's life. It is used in a variety of applications. This word is used both literally and figuratively. It is used proximate and remote. As follows, these are the things that are in the definition for hands: to be broken handed, consecrate, creditor, custody, debt, dominion, ministry, pain, sore, and terror.

The *Strong's* reference number for the word *hands* is 3027.

God commanded our hands to stay clean. What we do with them will determine our destiny. Your palms are a part of your hands. Whatever you use them to do sets the course for your life. Eve used her hands to rob God. She cursed the world and destroyed God's image, man. Adam agreed with her, instead of correcting her. This was the beginning of the shaking. The firmament would eventually break. The waters would come back together.

Adam's disobedience released an army of demons. Greed and lust would affect the entire globe. The human hands would do some horrible things. Satan would use our mind to bring forth evil. Palm readers and witches would arise. This is Jezebel's spirit controlling minds.

All things were affected according to the Hebrew term. Man was no longer consecrated. He was now set apart to be used by the devil. He lost his power and dominion to rule. He lost his fellowship and ministry with God. He would live under the curse of debt. He would owe everyone. He would stay in want until He put God first.

Dagon did not have feet. Jezebel did. This spirit is limited. It would soon blossom to the fullest. All it needed was human hands and feet. This would empower that spirit to travel. This spirit would destroy men through this woman. Here is that Scripture passage again. The

Hebrew definition for Jezebel's feet will follow. I will also give you the Hebrew definition for Jezebel's skull.

Second Kings 9:35 said they went to bury Jezebel, and they found no more of her than the skull, feet, and palms of her hands. The Hebrew word for Jezebel's feet is *regel* (reh'-gel). It makes reference to a foot or a person's feet when they are walking. It further implies that one is taking a step. The word *pudenda* is in this definition which refers to the sex organ of the male. The Strong's reference number for feet is 7272.

This word comes from the Hebrew word *ragal* (raw-gal). It makes reference to someone or something walking along. It describes the person as a tale bearer who slanders, backbites, and spies. The Strong's reference number for ragal is 7270.

When the serpent spirit gets your hands, it lays claim to your feet and entire body. His goal is to break your foot in the spirit realm and stop you from stepping into the place God wants you to rule in. This spirit wants to use the person that has disobeyed God but was never corrected. Most of all, these people are continually driven by deception and overtaken by pride.

This spirit entered in through the first woman. She tore her house down with her hands when she ate the forbidden fruit. Her husband agreed with her. His agreement left God without a face or an authoritative image to operate through. This is the beginning of what I refer to as "Mystery Babylon," a no-name society that will be born of this sin. These people will not want God's name.

Neither will they have the last name of their Father. This is the beginning of wickedness in high places. Unclean spirits will dominate the airways. Lust will cover the nations of the world. Many children will be products of their parents' affairs. They will not know their purpose in life.

In the Last Days, it will get worse. Men and women in Christianity will be stretched beyond their limits trying to minister to people who do not know why they were born. The world will be full of pain and people who do not respect human lives. This brings us to another stage of who Jezebel is.

Notice slander and backbiting are a part of Jezebel's feet. These are words of deception that are designed to destroy. This is the serpent waiting to work through someone who walks with you. I call it a snake that talked while Adam sat silent. The serpent will misguide your woman while you are standing there looking. This spirit will rob you blind and leave you crying. This happened to Adam and Eve. It also happened to Judas. All of this goes back to the serpent. He whispered words of deception to the woman. Now we are in a society where everyone is screaming something that is destructive.

In the beginning, Adam was supposed to rebuke the devourer serpent spirit of lust. Instead, that spirit used him to assist his wife when he knew better. God never planned things to go this way. Men and women have failed to cooperate with God. We now live in a society where men do not have fathers to speak into their lives.

*Two Thieves and a Yardstick*

Many do not know or have never seen their fathers. That absence in turn has caused children to hate God. The children despise the preacher that God wants to use as a father figure. Many children and adults do not respect anyone because they were wounded by their fathers.

God has always wanted to live in man. He placed them in authority in the beginning. They were supposed to lead and respect God's order concerning the forbidden fruit. Greed and lust released the spirit of Dagon and Jezebel. Notice the anointing on the ark cut Dagon's head off. It manifested again in Jezebel.

We have continued to disobey God's Spirit with our poor decisions. Instead of looking to God, many men have carved images and worshiped them. They have no idea that they are giving their authority over to another spirit. Man has chosen another God. He made his idols with his own hands. This is a picture of two spirits at war—God and the serpent, through man's flesh. Will God rule through man? Will man become his own god because of lust?

Satan is at work in the minds of the people. He will soon manifest in a women. She is a full-blown assassin. This is a serpent spirit at work in a woman. This raises two questions: Why does the Book of Revelation mention this dead woman again? What does she have to do with men and women today?

The Hebrew word for Jezebel's skull is *gulgoleth* (gul-go'-leth). It makes reference to the skull and speaks of something that's round, such as a person's head. It further states in enumerations of persons. This means name by name specifically as a list of people, the judgment of many is placed on this woman. The *Strong's* reference number 1538.

Jezebel destroyed many prophets. Every prophetic voice that she killed is being avenged. God placed it upon her head. Nothing is left except her skull, feet, and the palms of her hands. Her body is eaten up by the beast. This is what sin does to the body. It destroys. The beast, Satan, could no longer use that body. He will be waiting to find someone else. People die, but spirits do not. This means he is still using someone.

Her remains were evidence that the battle is not over. Nobody will be able to stand. God must now count up the cost. He will judge sin. He will bare our iniquities. He will judge the serpent. Mankind can receive the anointing that Adam lost. We will be left without an excuse.

This is why Jesus went to Golgotha in the New Testament. It is the place of the skull. He wants to empower mankind. This includes males and females. Once again the order will be set. The man will be in authority. His wife will possess the same power. He will cover her. She will be a helpmate. Both must decide what they will do about the fruit that God wants.

Following God's order will cause the nations to have holy fathers and disciplined men. Every man is the yardstick that his daughter needs. She can use his example to measure men. She will not have to pray long when a man finds her. The yardstick (her father) that she has will declare if he measures up or not.

Chapter 4

# THE TWO TOWERS

THIS CHAPTER WILL reveal the outcome of a society and government that reject God. This is the system that came as a result of Adam and his wife's sin. It has continued to this day because men do not know what seed God really wanted.

Our society and homes are a manifestation of what came out of Eve, the first pulpit. She is a picture of the church. Her body produced a devourer, or seedeater. We see it manifested when Cain kills Abel. Every since that day, the wrong kind of spirit has come out of the human body, or pulpit. We have produced children that hate God. Then we produced messages that tolerate our lust and greed. God's pulpit is defiled. The human body is broken and depraved. The church house and the government look the same way. And none of this will not stop until the family is re-established. This means one must legally get married. God forbid the fruit of the womb to be devoured. One must have a relationship with Jesus Christ. He is the true Vine that connects all creation back to God. You may read John, the fifteenth chapter.

The tower is a pulpit. The tower and the pulpit are buildings. The building is a picture of the first man and woman. This is the type of court system that came as a result of sin. It will reveal a people who do not want the name of God. It is the outcome of a government and society driven by selfishness, lust, and greed. Let's read on and hear the voice of the devourer. He uses men to build a city that dishonors God. The city is shaped and formed according to what is spoken from the tower. The tower pulpit does not belong to God because the people do not want or acknowledge God. Man has become the beast that speaks what he wants. His spirit is corrupt and his mind is confused. The work of the serpent is manifested in man. The flesh is greatly deceived and self-destructive when it does not want the spirit of God.

In Genesis 11:4–6, the people said, "Go to, let us build us a city and a tower, whose top may reach unto heaven; and let us make us a name, lest we be scattered abroad upon the face of the whole earth. And the LORD came down to see the city and the tower, which the children of men builded. And the LORD said, Behold, the people is one, and they have all one language; and this they begin to do: and now nothing will be restrained from them, which they have imagined to do." The Hebrew word for tower in these verses is *migdal* (mig-dawl), also (in plural) feminine *migdalah* (mig-daw-law), and it means a tower. By analogy the definition used the word *rostrum*. This means that the tower is similar to a plate form used for speaking publicly. The *Strong's* reference number 4026.

*The Two Towers*

The Hebrew word *migdal* (mig-dawl) comes from the Hebrew word *gadal* (gaw-dal). It is a primitive root and it means to twist, and at the same time make large. The definition specifically says to causatively make large in various sense, as in body, mind, estate, honor, and pride. The *Strong's* reference number for gadal (gaw-dal) is 1431.

The Lord came down to see the rostrum men had built. The rostrum is a place used for public speaking. God expected the rostrum to be a tower that would speak what He wanted. The people in the rostrum were supposed to stand up for Him. He expected them to operate with his mind. They appeared to be reaching up to heaven. At the same time they were breaking His rules.

Selfishness caused them to build themselves something other than what the Father commanded. This caused the rostrum to become twisted. The human mind operating in this rostrum was destroying itself. They honored themselves. They listened to their fleshly, corrupt desires. In their own sight, they were excellent. Everyone was happy with their name. Nobody had to answer to God. They could enlarge themselves in every sense. This mean whatever they said was the rule. Nobody could stop them. Self-destruction was setting in. The absence of God caused them to become confused.

This is the outcome of ignoring God. You cannot expect Him to show up when you have locked Him out. In the Last Days, we will see the mind of the government parallel to the rebellious nature of men and woman. It kills its babies legally.

In Genesis 11:7–9, God scattered the people. They were left confused. You cannot take God's rostrum and build yourself a name. It belongs to Him and your disobedience provokes God to respond according to how you live. This means lust and greed are causing us to hurt each other. It has not changed because we ignore God and do what we want.

In Genesis 11, God stopped the work of the people for their own good. I will show you how evil continued when mankind refused to submit. This same spirit manifested in the Book of Exodus. It operated in Pharaoh. This is the same devil operating in a new person. Evil continues because mankind and this government have refused God—and the same thing is happening today. The people in this nation continue to support and fight for everything God forbids.

In Genesis 11, I want you to focus on the fourth, fifth, and eighth verses. The Hebrew word for city will be the same in all three verses. Keep in mind these are the same verses we have discussed when we talked about the tower. It will reveal more about God's response to the people who have set up a government and a court system that has voted against His principles. This is a picture of a woman being used. It reveals what kind of sons and daughters she has given birth to. It is also a picture of a man who refuses to cover her and their children. This is what a broken government looks like because of selfish men and woman in the nation.

> And they said, Go to, let us build us a city and a tower, whose top may reach unto heaven; and let us make us a name, lest we be scattered abroad upon the face of the whole earth. And the LORD came down to see the city and the tower, which the children of men builded....So the LORD scattered them abroad from thence upon the face of all the earth: and they left off to build the city.
> —GENESIS 11:4–5, 8

The Hebrew word for city is *iyr* (eer), and it means a city (a place guarded by waking or a watch) that is a city guarded by someone that should be wide awake and fully alert. This word is used in the widest sense and makes reference to a court and a town. The *Strong's* reference number for the word *city* is 5892.

God came down to see the court system, town, and rostrum the children of men built. He saw who was guarding it. He knew who was watching over it. God concluded that they all had one language. They certainly were not speaking the things of God.

This they began to do. Nothing could restrain them. They would do whatever they imagined. Our response to God releases a judgment in return. Their lust brought them into confusion. No one could communicate. Everyone was forced to stop what they were doing. All should have recognized His name. They refused to honor God's name.

This is the result of Adam missing God's timing with the first woman. She is the first tower and rostrum, or pulpit. He named her after she sinned. She found out who she was after she was deceived. This becomes a picture of a government that does not know its assignment for God. It is also a picture of a woman who will get attacked and loses the men she needs to cover her.

In Exodus 1, confusion and miscommunication continue. A hardhearted beast is in the tower. He is a human being. He has the heart of a lion and a dragon at the same time. His goal is to cut off the male babies. He wants to use God's women to do it. The women feared God. At this time, the devourer did not have much assistance. The women chose to pray. His goal is to destroy any male figure because of the authority that a man represents.

This is a picture of the male lion in the animal kingdom. He uses the female. She is always left uncovered and can be mistreated. Her sons are put away by their father. They are never properly trained. They are often killed by other male lions. This forces them to hunt until they find a female that they can use. The cycle of the father never comes to an end.

This is the outcome of society. We have treated one another like animals due to lust and greed. It will not stop until men decide to stand against the seduction of women. The first woman caused this disorder. Adam never corrected her. Instead, he assisted her. Read on as I paint a picture for you.

The tower is a picture of a woman's body. Another spirit has entered into her. It is the spirit of the seed-eater. Right now, women who fear God surround her. These are woman who refuse to assist the devourer. One day, we will see the fullness of the society that she has given birth to. She will want nothing to do with God. It will be declared by her that He should not be acknowledged. She will despise women who pray. We will see her assist those with a hard heart. She will fall in love with the flesh. She will make homosexual lifestyles legal. She will give her consent for them to marry. She will kill her babies legally. This is a female taking on the mind of the dragon. It is the result of all nations because many men do not know what seed God wants.

Focus on Exodus 1:11. This verse tells us that God's people were forced to build treasure cities for Pharaoh. The Hebrew word for cities in this verse is the same as the word for *city*, which I just gave you. Demon activities increased because of a hardhearted ruler. They were making rules that did not honor God. Mankind is afflicting each other because of their own lust and greed. Read Exodus 1.

This is exactly what is happening today. God has always had a remnant that feared Him. The spirit of disorder wants to close all doors on God. Those in authority are hardhearted. The children are the ones who get killed or hurt. The family will eventually take on the mind of

Pharaoh. Nobody will force them to kill their sons. They will gladly kill their babies. It will be their choice and not the demands of the one in authority.

The government has been shaped by the family. This is the lion and the dragon at work. He has used men and women to destroy each other. Destruction has fallen on the children. Before it is over, the spirit of the beast will drown the cities. This will allow him to destroy a complete family, city, or nation at one time. If they live, they will be homeless, having nothing.

This is what Jezebel does when she gets in the water. She takes your prosperity and causes a flood. She has no respect for anyone. This spirit is after blood.

Let's continue with Exodus 1. I will give you a Hebrew word for treasure. I told you the people built treasure cities for Pharaoh. This is a picture of what Pharaoh wants. It is a picture of a Jezebel spirit. We do not respect the human body or protect it. It is a picture of a city in disorder because a hardhearted man is in authority.

In Exodus 1:11, the Hebrew word for treasure is *mickenah* (mis-ken-aw). It is defined as a magazine and a store (-house). The Strong's reference number for treasure is 4543. This word comes from the Hebrew word *kanac* (kaw-nas), a primitive root which means to collect, to enfold, or gather (together). The *Strong's* reference number for kanac (kaw-nas) is 3664. Pharaoh afflicted God's people, making them build treasure cities for him. The midwives were oppressed by him. He did not want any praying women around. His goal was to

*The Two Towers*

destroy every male child. He understood the authority that men carry. He would have to kill them before they were mature. He wanted the praying women to assist him in this slaughter.

Take notice of the word *magazine*, which is a part of the definition for the word *treasure*. What does all of this mean? Read on as I reveal what kind of treasure city he made the people build for him. I will also show you how this will fully blossom in the Last Days.

The word *magazine* is defined as a place where things are stored such as a warehouse. The world is filled with all kinds of magazines. Sometimes the magazine is referred to as a storehouse or a building. Its purpose is to house explosive material or other items that can be bought or sold. The armed forces have a magazine. It is sometimes referred to as a military supply depot. At times ammunition is hidden in a fort or on a warship. This ship is just like a massive weapon ready to destroy its enemy. Like a gun that has a chamber, the bullets are held until the time of release. A magazine is also a paperback publication that has stories and pictures. It usually shows advertisements or gives information about something or someone.

This is the kind of city that has come as a result of a hard heart. Right now it is a picture of one man. His name is Pharaoh. He is in authority. This man has the heart of a dragon. His massive killing has begun. He is killing all of the male babies. This is a man with a Jezebel spirit. The people are forced to build the city the way

Pharaoh wants it to be. This is his definition of a treasure city. In the Last Days, the spirit of the dragon will increase. This is when the spirit of Pharaoh will manifest to the fullest. Governments and regions will fight each other. Nations and kingdoms will be territorial. There will be no order in the nations of the world. The blood of our men continually screams from the ground. First, it was the children. Today, it is the fathers.

These things came as a result of the first family. Greed and lust has forced us to treat each other like enemies. The human mind has become selfish and savage. Nobody understands that selfishness and lust did this to the world that God wanted for Himself. Nobody wants God. Many men do not acknowledge Him. Greed and lust are ruling the atmosphere. Adam gave the princes (all men) to the spirit of Babylon. Many princes will live like there is no God. Their spirit will dominate the atmosphere. When Babylon gets through, he will bring the globe to ground zero. This is when the drowning starts.

Take notice of the definition for *magazine*. It is no longer just explosive military ammunition used on the front line. The magazines have expanded to include poison, such as *Playboy* and *Penthouse*. You can now get things legally on video. It can also be downloaded on the Internet. The warehouse and the storehouse are filled with this stuff. These magazines are mass weapons that are killing our men. These books and movies are a sure sign that shows men and women are willingly destroying each other because of lust and greed.

## The Two Towers

The government has approved it. They have embraced it. Or as the definition says, they have enfolded it. Just like pharaoh. They are waiting to collect. How many men will die? Has anyone lead them to Christ? Is the nation praying at all? When will the nations turn to God? What will the beast use mankind to do next? I warn this nation now—cease from self-destruction before it is too late!

This shows me that all have been attacked by the lion spirit, or Satan. We have also become the lion because we are hardhearted. Satan cannot do anything without a body to work through. This means every man has a will. God cannot help you if you refuse to give in to Him.

In this hour, there are two towers, or pulpits. One is the voice that comes from the church. The other is the voice of the world government. Both have compromised. This is why we cannot figure out what happened on 9/11.

Those in authority are being challenged to change. God want His order to be set. We cannot vote on issues God has already settled. It will open a door for humanity to be cursed. Adam and Eve are the beginning of God's government. The church and the government were one in the beginning. It is a picture of one man and one woman. Their disobedience caused all men to be attacked and cursed. It continues because humanity is lustful, selfish, and greedy.

God gave us Jesus. The government was upon His shoulders. This is a picture of God bringing all humanity back to Himself. It is up to mankind to agree with God.

Ignoring God leaves the world uncovered. You will see how cruel the human flesh can become when we do not want Him. The atmosphere is filled with the spirit of the devourer. This is the serpent spirit operating in many men. Women are running around naked and homeless. They are being attacked by the serpent spirit that lives in many men. The serpent spirit is also causing women to seduce men. Lust and greed are everywhere. Men and women are hurting each other and God. Once again I hear God saying, "Sound the alarm!"

God put man in authority. He told him to take dominion. Many have fallen into lust, yet refuse correction. Man curses at God and afflicts others with his words. God is setting the judgment and looking at the calendar. He is waiting on you to cry out because He loves you, even in the middle of your sins.

Judgment is not God attacking humanity. It is the consequence that comes from our personal choices. God has given us His Word. We know what He expects of us. He desires all to choose life, to choose Him. Rejecting Him leaves you undisciplined and greedy. Your selfishness will leave a trail of blood behind you. It is the same trail that someone left you in.

Blood and iniquity are all around us. Many are following the iniquities of the previous generation. God loves you. He commands you to be free in Jesus' name.

Earlier we talked about the young lion. I told you it also refers to a group of houses knitted together. The houses are larger than a village and smaller than a city or town. It is also a community incorporated as a municipality, which is a city or town that has its own incorporated government.

We have ignored this spirit when it was a young lion. He invaded our classrooms. Our children were murdered. He has opened fire in daycare centers. The little babies were killed. In the past few years or decades, he has been operating on the college campuses. He is taking our young sons and daughters before they can get married or even give birth. Did you notice he has taken a few teachers and college professors as well? He is determined to leave a family fatherless and without a mother. He has assassinated many presidents. How was the first assassination connected to the lion and the spirit of prostitution?

We have completely ignored this spirit. Can anyone hear God's cry? The young lion has opened fire in the courtrooms. The nations are in trouble. Men and women are hurt and angry. This is the result of God's fatherhood being lost in the Garden of Eden.

The spirit of the young lion is in its final stage. He is fully developed. This spirit is more progressive. It has now put on the mind of the dragon. This is when the bottomless pit begins and destruction is inevitable.

The word *lion* means "to be fierce." The word *fierce* means "to have a violently cruel nature." It also means "to be wild, uncontrolled, and distasteful." This beast stepped into the globe when the first family sinned. He claimed God's princes before they were ever born. This spirit now lives inside mankind. Humanity has become the devourer.

The lion spirit has prevailed because of lust, greed, and disorderly people. The lion is no longer just in the town and cities where we live. It is everywhere. He wants all creation. He is attacking the government. The government is a picture of a woman without a man of God over her.

She has everyone's children while their fathers run wild. She is also a picture of what a woman condones when the men are not in their place; a picture of a woman who is lost without God and she does not even realize it. She is a woman who determines the rise or fall of a nation.

What has she been faced with since the fall of Adam? Her daughters have been raped and used. Some have no husbands. This has caused her to condone abortion. They have asked her for permission. She has granted it. This is a direct attack against God. Her sons have no fathers. Some of them have children by many different women. She has been taking care of the babies. Now she has to chase him down for money. He has become selfish and greedy. He declares that he is not the father. Maybe he is not, but her daughters do not know. God is not pleased. What are we going to do? The entire globe must repent. All have robbed God.

This woman is in trouble. Her sons now struggle. They are tormented about their sexuality. They want her permission to legally marry a man. Once again she

## The Two Towers

has granted it. In some places she will not allow it. But, her children are crying for it. What is the church going to do?

The government is a picture of a woman without God. She has no direction without God's man. She is being led by the serpent spirit. God is calling for the globe to travail for her. This raises one question: Who will God use to call the globe unto repentance? This person is chosen. God will use him to minister healing to every face.

The globe is already in travail. Everything we built is crumbling. It is not the devil this time. God wants an image. This hour is about the face of God. Men have been used by women. Many women have used their money to control men. Many men have used women. They have used money to buy sex. The globe does not completely possess the heart of a father. Men are angry and have not always been honored. Some have not walked in a respectable manner. Every man has done something that he is ashamed of.

Every man is created with a purpose from God. He loves all men. There are so many children born out of wedlock. Teenage pregnancy is everywhere. This is the spirit of Jezebel at work. The entire world has robbed God. The gospel has not been really preached. This is why religious people feel comfortable in sin. Ignorance has caused many to worship idols. This is no different than the Philistines who worshipped Dagon. He is the fish god they made with their hands.

God is still grieved. He will not be relieved until this government turns. It is not enough for the church to be saved. Jesus had the government upon His shoulders. Jesus did not die to leave it in disorder. This means the church better go to war on their faces. We must fight until the globe goes into an eternal travailing. Warning! Travail!

Everything that the Christian is going through is not from the devil. God is calling us to deny ourselves. We must take up our cross and follow Him. We are nailed to it by denying the flesh of its cravings. The Word of God is the hammer and nails that will kill our old desires. This is a daily experience. We cannot afford to compromise.

Our homes are out of order. The church is out of order. This government is out of order. This has taken place because many men are out of order. They are fighting for honor from their wives. They are trying to get something that they have not given to God. You cannot be first. Your wife cannot, either.

God wants the mind of Christ to operate in men and women. Peace will return when we get rid of selfishness. Lust and greed has eaten up our marriages. Divorce will stop when we seek God's face.

The two towers—pulpits—that were attacked on 9/11 reminded me of husbands and wives. Both can stand if only one is attacked. God will restore all. Nothing will be lost. Who can God work through when both collapse? This means everything in you is lost.

Everything happening is a result of selfishness and

greed. It could be the assassins in the planes on 9/11. Maybe it is a husband and wife. It could be this world's government. Everybody is trying to get something. Our approach on how to get it is not always the best. People are dying and getting hurt. This is what happens when nobody wants God.

May I ask everyone a question? Who cares? I do not mean, "Who cares?" I am talking about, "Do you care?" The globe has had a "so what" attitude. Many do not care because they are hurt. This is the time to care. God is turning one more time. He is giving us His face. Fathers and sons will be healed. A global gathering will take place. Get ready for your next level of living.

As I close out this chapter, I want to help everyone understand the hour that we are in. Psalm 24:1 says, "The earth is the LORD's, and the fulness thereof; the world, and they that dwell therein." This is a mindboggling scripture. The lust and greed of man has locked God out of the earth that belonged to Him from the beginning. There is no room for Him in our homes. The church is slowly pushing Him out. Man has locked Him out of the nations of the world. When He knocks, no one will let Him in.

Nobody will put up with this for long. They will feel less than who they are. Their habits cause them to question their ability to help you. Then Satan will accuse them for what happens to them. It is actually your fault when you reject the one who came to help you. This is what happened to God. He has been locked out of our homes and the nation. Rebellion has left the family without God. What happens when God cries? What happens when wives or husbands cry? Have you ever cried? You wanted something to happen and it did not? You did everything and someone refused to turn? This will release a judgment toward the person. When judgment comes, this means a person will suffer the consequences of their own choices only because they were unwilling to change.

Chapter 5

# I DON'T FEEL LIKE A MAN IN MY OWN HOUSE

God gave His Son for the entire world. His arms are open for anyone who chooses Him. The spirit of the thief has remained in this world. He operates through men and women. The beast, the nature of the devil, has been ruling God's government since the fall of Adam. God sent His Son to demonstrate His divine order. Jesus came to set the government free from her lust. This government is all of humanity, who has voted against Him. This has left them wounding each other because of deception and greed.

Jesus came to show men how to submit to the Father. He gives them back their position as men of authority. Then He steps back once again, allowing them to choose. His desire is for them to bring healing to the government. They will do that by making their relationships legal in His sight. One man should have one woman legally. When lust and greed enter, you can expect the government to break down. She will be left with a lot of children without any fathers for them. This is a picture of women as the government as we see it today.

We have ignored the example of Jesus. He shows a man how to submit to his Father. Then He demonstrated the love a man should have for his wife. He should become willing to be a sacrifice for her. His wife becomes his helpmate. She has a mind to submit knowing she will not be abused. His love transforms her into the image God wanted from the beginning. Healing comes to the government because we respect God's order. This is the power of love when two people understand that they cannot eat the forbidden fruit.

Lust robbed the kingdom from the beginning. It has left us fatherless. Mothers have been mistreated. Children have been left in the orphanage. It continually produces a generation that will have marriages that will not last. This is why Jesus cried out for oneness in the New Testament. He understood that a son cannot function properly without the guidance of his father. Jesus also knew that a father cannot properly lead his son without a relationship with God. He became the example of true submission. This means a son surrenders all to God. Then the son must be lead by his father's spirit.

This is where we continue to lose the battle. Nobody wants God. What is even worse is that we have fathers leading us that have the wrong spirit. They have given their sons permission to freely use women. A son is not ready for marriage until he has been prepared by his father. How can this happen when men keep having children by women that they are not married to? This means the man will not be in the home to train the child the way God wanted. A woman is not ready to submit because she did not have a father in the home to submit to. This is why the church is so necessary. It is up to the church to prepare grown-up adults for their purpose in God. It must also prepare them for marriage. These are things that many adults did not get in their childhood.

Many sons and daughters have had fathers who abused them. It may have been physically with the hands or emotionally because he was absent. Maybe it was verbal abuse. Many children watched their father curse at their mother. Nobody told these men they were training their daughters and grooming their sons. It has caused women to tolerate abuse from someone who said, "I'm never going to change." It has groomed sons into becoming the men they said they would never be.

Now, many women are angry and cold. This is why men do not feel like a man in their own homes. They are feeling the same devastation that God is experiencing. Your wife cannot give you something that you have not given to God. This means a man must repent and become willing to give himself completely to God for the woman he desires. It also means a woman must honor and help the man whom God is using to cover her.

It is important for pastors to help their members understand the commitment they have as members. They are obligated to pray for members and their spouses. Their love should be pure. Pastors are placed in members' lives as a covering and a shield. Nobody has ever said that pastors are positioned to help members get what their parents failed to give them. Many times, the members are allowed to drift along and draw from their leaders. They have not been equipped on how to guard their leaders and discern when the atmosphere is too heavy for the man and woman in the house.

God forbid the members sit down and not know that their house of God needs their prayers. How can we go into a house that blesses us and not cover it? I rebuke it and command it to stop. It is time for members to pray for their leaders. Remember, they have the responsibility of your destiny, while also being husbands, wives, and parents to their own families.

As I continue in this chapter, I will go back into some Old Testament scriptures. It will reveal what happens when the Holy Spirit has to fight against the flesh of a stubborn individual. This will show how lust causes the imagination of men to run wild. Men and women will agree on everything dishonorable that they can think of. Man will eventually become his own God. He will be unable to experience lasting joy and peace. It is the outcome of pride and arrogance. Valuing our own opinion and ignoring God has left us hopelessly marrying four and five times.

Two people must become willing to submit to God concerning the forbidden fruit. We are incomplete without one another. It is not good for man to be alone. It is not good for a woman to be left uncovered. In the first chapter, I asked what God really wanted from Adam. Here is the answer. I will explain the Hebrew definition. Psalm 127:3 says, "Lo, children are an heritage of the LORD: and the fruit of the womb is his reward." The Hebrew word for heritage is *nachalah* (nakh-al-aw). It means something inherited such as an heirloom or an estate. This Hebrew word also means patrimony which is property passed down to a son from his father. The *Strong's* reference number for the word *heritage* is 5159.

The only thing God wanted from Adam is a family. Children are an heirloom to God. They are His priceless personal property. God gave Adam everything. Adam inherited the globe. He is placed in authority by God. Everything God has is given to Adam. He is given authority with the responsibility of protecting God's heirlooms. This would be the beginning of God's government and the family. It would be the beginning of parenthood and one nation under God. Nobody would be raped, used, sold like a slave, or abused.

Adam became lustful and greedy. He gave away God's heirloom, all humanity. This would be the beginning of confusion and rebellion. The human mind would become wicked and depraved. Men and women would not value marriage or having a family the way God wanted. Their definition of an heirloom would be an important piece of furniture or perhaps a piece of jewelry from grandmother. They would fight to keep old items in the family, and at the same time place absolutely no value on human lives.

Many men understand that God place them in authority. They will remind you that they are the head. They are even praying for God's favor. Yet, they have ignored and despised the heirloom called children. Nobody has trained them to keep the heirloom in one family. Once again, lust and greed are the problems. Men and women have failed to help each other. God is pulling back His eternal curtain. He wants us to see His face.

This is what it means to sow to your flesh. Eating the forbidden fruit causes us to reap corruption. Earlier, I asked, "Who cares?" I come to tell you, God cares! This world is a picture of what men and women have done to each other. The fatherhood of God was disrupted when the forbidden fruit was eaten. It determined how Adam felt about being a father. He proved to be undisciplined. Adam gave away God's heirlooms. He separated the kingdom that God wanted to come to all humanity. This is the beginning of a no-name society.

The world will have fatherless children. They will be hungry and angry. The world is filled with God's heirlooms. They do not know that they belonged to God from the beginning.

God's Spirit does not have an image. The face of God—mankind—is abusing the authority of God. Many men have become wild and lustful. I warn the entire globe: God is calling for His face, every man!

Let's go back to an Old Testament scripture. This will reveal the mind of the people after Adam's fall. The mind of humanity is the same today. We have taken our lives and did what we want. Out of the blackness of our hearts, we have produced all kinds of evil.

In Genesis 6:3, the Lord said, "My spirit shall not always strive with man, for that he also is flesh: yet his days shall be an hundred and twenty years." The Hebrew word for flesh in this verse is the same as the word *flesh* when Adam said the woman is, "flesh of my flesh." God expected the family to be one and cover each other. Ever since Adam's Fall, men have done anything they wanted sexually. They have failed to guard the womb of the female. The woman is at fault just as much as the man. God will not continue to compete with our flesh. He will not watch you produce children out of your affairs. God forbid you to fall into lust and destroy His portion.

Every man is supposed to produce children by his own spouse. God gave us Christ so that we can be brought back to God as sons and daughters. The Spirit of Christ is now at work in men. Christ is at work in women, too. He expects the man to uphold His standards. His Word empowers you to teach your own children about Him. You are a priest and God holds you responsible for your children. Everyone must pray because some men have children by many women. We must also remember this is not about beating our men or women up. Adam and Eve just messed us up, but Christ restored us. Now we must refresh our definition of love.

God will also cause many to give money from the north, east, south, and west. We will rebuild nations.

Everyone will have a place to stay. All will know that God loves them. It will be the love we share that will change angry lives.

Some have children by other women. Many women have children by another man. You are now with a new person. How do you handle it? Genesis 6:5–7 says, "And God saw that the wickedness of man was great in the earth, and that every imagination of the thoughts of his heart was only evil continually. And it repented the Lord that he had made man on the earth, and it grieved him at his heart. And the Lord said, I will destroy man whom I have created from the face of the earth; both man, and beast, and the creeping thing, and the fowls of the air; for it repenteth me that I have made them." The Hebrew definitions for these three words (thought, repented, grieved) reveal the work of the beast operating in man once Adam sinned. The very thoughts of men were evil continually. They carried out everything their imagination could think of. This grieved God. Their wickedness pushed them away from Him. It repented God. He refused to compete with their flesh.

Here is the first Hebrew definition. The Hebrew word for grieved is *atsab* (aw-tsab), and the *Strong's* reference number for the word *grieved* is 6087. It refers to displeasure, pain, and anger. There are three words in the longer definition that I will comment on. The words *carve*, *fabricate*, and *wrest*. All three have one thing in common, the pressure that must be applied in order for each word to manifest its definition in the truest sense.

## I Don't Feel Like a Man in My Own House

The chipping and cutting process is always used when something is being carved. During the carving process fabrication takes place. This means something is being formed while it is being built. Violence and twisting takes place, which are part of the definition for the word *wrest*. The object now takes on the form that the instrument is forming it into. These actions are always used to change the true nature and meaning of something that already exists. Lust in the garden is the beginning of these allegations. God has been attacked by humanity. This is the work of the serpent operating in mankind. This is now the sixth chapter of Genesis. The separation between God and man has continued.

There are other words used to describe the word *wrest*. The first word is *distort*. The second one is *usurp*. When something is distorted, you can no longer recognize what it is. When you usurp authority over someone or something, it means the person in authority operates in the position illegally. The person is also cruel having no one to correct them. Lust and greed did this to the globe. It has caused men and women to disrespect each other and God.

Mankind grieved God with their ways. Their abuse caused God to question whether to help them. This is one of the worse things any man can feel. He has what it takes to fix the situation. Nobody wants to give in to what is right. This will force them to repent. (They are forced to turn from the person that refuses correction.)

The abuse of mankind aggrieved God's heart. They

treated Him like they were God. Their lust pushed them away from Him. They did not understand their purpose for living. Their earthly bodies are supposed to be His house. The human body and soul are supposed to be where God's Spirit dwells. The breath of life is the measure of faith God has given to every man. The family has been born in sin ever since Adam's lust. Humanity has the unclean nature of their fathers. This has caused men to reproduce wickedness. It continually leads the next generation away from God. Now humanity questions if God exist. Their minds have become contaminated, diseased, and unprotected, just like a womb that has been left uncovered and abused.

The human mind has conceived many thoughts and carried them out. When you watch what man produces, it is a sure sign that he is being pulverized by the serpent spirit. This means that his flesh is being attacked, diminished, and left lifeless. It will do anything when the mind of God is not operating inside of us.

God is grieved in the presence of man. He knew how lustful the flesh could be when He is absent. God was being twisted, smothered, and run out of the house that is supposed to be His temple.

The very thoughts of men are wicked to the bones. God did not create man to abuse each other. He certainly will not tolerate being abused. God is not in a battle, at all. He could have forced man to turn. Who wants love like that? God certainly did not. This is exactly what is happening in marriages. We are twisting and putting pressure on our partners. We are craving things that God forbids. Our thoughts are wicked, with a determination to carry out those desires. We refuse to receive discipline and cast out those thoughts every time they come up.

God gave man a helpmate. It is time to help each other. This means someone must remain stable in order for the relationship to work. Two people must choose to love and obey God. Both will lose when everyone leaves God.

In Genesis 6:5–7, God is grieved to His heart. I gave you the Hebrew word for heart in the second chapter. I told you the heart of man, the heart of God, and the heart of Pharaoh all had the same definition. It deals with the feelings, the will, and intellect. It also means to care for, comfort, and consider. The words *stiff*, *stout*, and *double-hearted* are included.

Mankind's actions repented God. Their actions changed His feelings, mind, and will. He is brokenhearted inside of the body that is supposed to be His dwelling place. Man chose to be divided from God. They wanted Him their own way. The people would not give in. God was disrespected.

Men have always cried for God's help. When He shows up, they refuse to do it His way. This will always cause them to question themselves about things God is ready to fix. Situations in life remain broken because we will not allow God to fix them according to His Word. This raises one question: What happens when God is repented? I will answer this question now. It will reveal the defeat of a marriage. It will reveal the defeat of man's relationship with God. Most of all, it will reveal the drowning and destruction of all human lives.

We cannot expect to win when we refuse to do things God's way. Men must operate with the mind of God if they expect a woman to submit. God never gave a man the right to lead His daughters away from Him. He also never wanted a woman to run out of His presence when she must be led by the man and corrected if she is wrong.

Let's look at that Scripture passage again. Keep in mind, this is an Old Testament scripture. It will reveal how wicked men were. This same wickedness remains today. It continues because we ignore God. Humanity has been selfish, greedy, and undisciplined.

In Genesis 6:5–7, it reads, "And God saw that the wickedness of man was great in the earth, and that every imagination of the thoughts of his heart was only evil continually. And it repented the Lord that he had made man on the earth, and it grieved him at his heart. And the Lord said, I will destroy man whom I have created from the face of the earth; both man, and beast, and the creeping thing, and the fowls of the air; for it repenteth me that I have made them." The Hebrew word for repented is *nacham* (naw-kham), and is *Strong's* reference number 5162. It refers to breathing strongly, or by implication to be sorry. And, God Himself began to, in fact, breathe strongly. He was sorry, and it was in a favorable sense. He is getting ready to ease Himself. He wanted the best for His children. There is nothing He would not have done for them. God had suffered long. His love forever remains. This is a one-sided relationship. Nobody could see that unconditional love demands the other party to change. There will be a judgment when you choose to be inconsiderate.

This is exactly what is happening in marriages. We want to do what we want. We have demanded respect that we have not given in return. Many have watched their spouses deny themselves. They have remained godly and prayed for you. Their sacrifice for you became an act of abuse.

This means, if one spouse has done what it takes for both of them to live, they will not continue to bleed because the other will not give up their will. A person in a struggle has to become willing to take instructions. You cannot do what you want and tell your spouse to mind his or her own business. Doing so may leave you to be processed by God without the assistance of your spouse. I warn you. It will not be easy.

We are still in Genesis 6:5–7. The Hebrew word for thoughts is *machashabah* (makh-ash-aw-baw) or *machashebeth* (makh-ash-eh-beth), from *Strong's* reference number 4284. It refers to imagination or purposeful intellectual activity. Man's thoughts were evil continually. Their mind set is working like a machine. He has a contrivance that is concrete. This means he has power to think up a plan. It could be good or evil. Schemes and tricks are included.

Mankind is in a fixed state. They wanted nothing to do with God. They were determined to carry out the evil they have contemplated. Mankind was hooked on their flesh. God refused to compete with people who chose to rebel.

Genesis 6:8 says, "Noah found grace in the eyes of the LORD." Genesis 6:9–12 tells us that Noah was just and perfect in his generation. He walked with God. He had three sons. The earth was corrupt. It was full of violence. All flesh had corrupted God's way. God would not continue to compete with mankind's flesh. In Genesis 6:13–17, God said to Noah, "The end of all flesh is come before me; for the earth is filled with violence through them; and, behold, I will destroy them with the earth. Make thee an ark of gopher wood; rooms shalt thou make in the ark, and shalt pitch it within and without with pitch. And this is the fashion which thou shalt make it of: The length of the ark shall be three hundred cubits, the breadth of it fifty cubits, and the height of it thirty cubits. A window shalt thou make to the ark, and in a cubit shalt thou finish it above; and the door of the ark shalt thou set in the side thereof; with lower, second, and third stories shalt thou make it. And, behold, I, even I, do bring a flood of waters upon the earth, to destroy all flesh, wherein is the breath of life, from under heaven; and every thing that is in the earth shall die." Genesis 6:18–20 reads, "But with thee will I establish my covenant; and thou shalt come into the ark, thou, and thy sons, and thy wife, and thy sons' wives with thee. And of every living thing of all flesh, two of every sort shalt thou bring into the ark, to keep them alive with thee; they shall be male and female. Of fowls after their kind, and of cattle after their kind, of every creeping thing of the earth after his kind, two of every sort shall come unto thee, to keep them alive."

Noah built the ark as God required. He followed all instructions. I am sure many had the opportunity to hear Noah's warning. In Genesis 7:1–2, the Lord told Noah to go into the ark with his family. He told Noah to bring seven of every clean beast, male and female, and the beasts that are not clean, the male and his female, to take two of each. In Genesis 7:4, 6–7, God said, "For yet seven days, and I will cause it to rain upon the earth forty days and forty nights; and every living substance that I have made will I destroy from off the face of the earth....And Noah was six hundred years old when the flood of waters was upon the earth. And Noah went in, and his sons, and his wife, and his sons' wives with him, into the ark, because of the waters of the flood."

Let's look in the New Testament. I want to show you how repentance works for a sinner. I want to show you how God was repented. This is terrible. What does it feel like to be the Savior, yet you are treated like the sinner? How could this awesome God take what men dished out?

Second Corinthians 7:10 tells us, "Godly sorrow worketh repentance to salvation." Sorrow is not just crying tears. It is a conviction that opens the eyes to the truth. The person becomes brokenhearted. He is willing to turn from sin. God gives him a new heart and mind. This is through knowledge of the Word. The person is made into a strong weapon. You will speak the Word of God when you are tempted. God will honor it because He cannot lie.

In Genesis, mankind refused to honor God. This repented the Father. He did not just cry tears. He was brokenhearted. God spoke the word and it came to pass because He cannot lie. In Genesis 7:11–12, the fountains of the great deep were broken up. The windows of heaven were opened. The Word of God tells us it rained. God told me this was not just rain. They were His tears. It took Him forty days to get it out. He went into travailing, strong crying, and mourning. Tears of sorrow always accompany repentance.

God loved His people. He wanted them to stay, but He could not get anything He deserved or desired out of them. God was totally dishonored. All mankind was destroyed. He preserved Noah and His family in the ark.

Let's look back at Noah's ark in Genesis 6:14. I want to compare it to the word *ark* in Exodus 2:3–5. Moses' mother built an ark. Both have the same definitions. The Hebrew word for ark is *tebah* (tay-baw), *Strong's* reference number 8392. Noah obeyed God. Moses' mother had to obey God. Both had to build the ark the way God wanted. Their obedience to God kept them from the assassin. Their families were preserved, also. God has always been trustworthy. He has always protected anyone who was willing to obey. God has a plan for every person. Rebellion will lead to the destruction of you and your children.

From the time of the Book of Genesis to this very day, mankind has rebelled. God forever seeks His children. He wants a people who will operate with His mind. He desires a bride who can be trusted. Male and female are the brides God wants. He has given His anointing to us. This anointing is Christ. It is time for us to be the ark that God's presence can live in. We are the ark that will be used to rescue our families and others.

We are in the Last Days. God is not waiting for someone to give Him back His house. He will interrupt our religious services. Every idol will be knocked down. Our lifestyles have provoked this type of response. Nobody will be able to stop what is about to take place.

God wants the nations of the world. He wants this government. Everything is coming back to Him. All have to choose. Nobody will play church any more. We will love God or the waters will rule the globe. We cannot blame God for the lust we enjoy. Eating the forbidden fruit leaves God without a face. This raises one question: What happens when God does not have a face?

God is a Spirit. Darkness covered the ground. Who is darkness, anyway? Darkness wanted the face in the ground. God moved on the first day of Creation. He separated darkness from light. Darkness really wanted to fight. Darkness loves destruction. Darkness wanted to slaughter. Darkness wanted the man out of the way. Darkness wanted the waters. Who are the waters, anyway? Why did water cover the ground? Let me give you a poem and a riddle. This is the second day of Creation, mind you:

> God separated the waters from the waters.
> He put a firmament in the sky.
> In the beginning, the waters had a face.
> Nobody would ever die.
> The waters are oh, so, precious.
> In the beginning they covered the ground.
> The waters just needed a belly.
> Then the water would return to the ground.
> Nobody will ever get raped.
> Darkness will never rule.
> This is what God planned.
> He gave man a right to choose.
> Nobody will ever be homeless.
> God is the Father of all.

The forbidden fruit will determine the outcome. Eating it will release a spirit of Babylon. Tell me, who is the "Mystery Babylon"? What does Babylon have to do with a flood? (Jezebel is in the water.) It is all about the blood.

Chapter 6

# THROWING THE BABY OUT WITH THE BATH WATER

WHAT IS GOD's definition of a bride? What does the bride have to do with the waters? Why must the waters be protected by the bride? Who is the bride, anyway? The bride is the church. Where was the church in the beginning? The first man and the woman were the church. I know this seems mind-boggling, but God wants me to untie the knot.

The mind and our marriages are in a mess. That is why the flesh has begun to rot. The nations and our marriages are experiencing the curse. Genesis 1:1–5 says, "In the beginning God created the heaven and the earth. And the earth was without form, and void; and darkness was upon the face of the deep. And the Spirit of God moved upon the face of the waters. And God said, Let there be light: and there was light. And God saw the light, that it was good: and God divided the light from the darkness. And God called the light Day, and the darkness he called Night. And the evening and the morning were the first day." God was about to create a man, He wanted a picture of Himself. Darkness would never enter the land. Man was never to know evil. God knew it would ruin the plan. God would create a human body. Then, God's Spirit would live in the man.

Tell me, who or what is darkness? Why is it separated from the light? Tell me, who is Jezebel? When did she enter the fight? Tell me, who is the face in the deep? Did it ever become a man? Why did the waters and Spirit surround the man? Let's look deeper into God's plan.

In Genesis 2:7 it says, "The LORD God formed man of the dust of the ground, and breathed into his nostrils the breath of life; and man became a living soul." God's body is in parts. It will first need a head. This is only the start. He formed a body from the ground. This body is a man. Adam's face is in the deep. Now the face is a man. God formed this body. This body is God's house. This body is God's mansion. Another mansion is in that house. Adam will be processed. God will give him a bride. He must first be tested. Remember God lives inside.

The squeezing process will begin. Who will be the boss? Adam must simply deny himself. That was the only cost. The Father instructed Adam. He also gave him a choice. Adam has a will. God needed a voice. God's Spirit is holy. He wanted the waters to come down. (Adam's belly will release them.) The globe will not drown.

Genesis 2:18–20 says, "And the LORD God said, It is not good that the man should be alone; I will make him an help meet for him. And out of the ground the LORD

God formed every beast of the field, and every fowl of the air; and brought them unto Adam to see what he would call them: and whatsoever Adam called every living creature, that was the name thereof. And Adam gave names to all cattle, and to the fowl of the air, and to every beast of the field; but for Adam there was not found an help meet for him." Adam is alone. He is about to become a groom. His body is God's mansion. This mansion is God's room. Inside the mansion is a bride. She is with God in this room. His Spirit will not release her. God is still inspecting the room. He is checking the DNA. The spirit is observing Adam's heart. God is searching for any evidence. Eating forbidden fruit will drive Him out. The mansion is spick and span. God is happy in this room. The groom is given one more assignment. Then his bride will come out of the room.

He was assigned to name the beast. This will cause them to submit. God knew the power of disorder. This spirit (of disorder) could be a trip. God has given the man His authority. Adam's mouth is the key. He will speak like his Father. There will be no disease. God's Spirit is in that body. He is prepared to agree with man. God wants him to rule the serpent spirit. He did not want that spirit to rule the man. Adam is wonderfully made. He is also one with God. Together they are treading on the serpent spirit. The serpent is under the feet of the man of God.

> And the LORD God caused a deep sleep to fall upon Adam and he slept: and he took one

of his ribs, and closed up the flesh instead thereof.
—Genesis 2:21

The groom is put to sleep. His mind is set toward the sky. There was no such thing as a bachelor's party. This groom is really fly. He has the Spirit and mind of his Father. His Father's Spirit will run his house. He was born with his Father's Spirit. It will dominate the land and his house. God is doing a work. He did not want the ground or woman abused. This is why He tested Adam. This man of God has been approved. God's Spirit is protecting Adam. He did not want Adam to bleed. The ground is a picture of man. Adam came from the ground indeed. The ground is the first womb. It is a reflection of the man. There will never be a volcano or floodwaters. If there are, something has erupted in man.

As you know, they ate the forbidden fruit. This is the beginning of many floods. The Jezebel spirit entered in. Lust contaminated the blood. This spirit is killing women. It is destroying so many men. Jezebel is gone wild. The globe is a lion's den. God did not come to condemn us. God forbade us to give up. God does not want us to give up. God loves everyone. He is calling for all. The Father's mantle is being dropped. "Mystery Babylon" claimed us all.

Adam threw the babies out. The kingdoms are being drowned. Eve was supposed to crown Adam. She gave Babylon his crown. The serpent started talking. That is how Babylon entered in. Adam never opened his mouth.

The globe became the lion's den. Adam never silenced the serpent. He allowed him to speak out. He should have prophesied to the wind. I will tell you later what that is about. The Book of Revelation talks about a woman. In her hand is a golden cup. This woman is sitting upon many waters. Who is this woman with this cup?

It is all about the blood. Why are we having so many floods? Where did Adam get his crown? What are the crowns doing now?

Chapter 7

## THERE'S A LION IN THE HOUSE AND HE MUST GO!

EVERY MAN AND woman is getting ready to cry. We have no fellowship with God the Father. Humanity lives as though there is no God. The land will be filled with darkness. Adam destroyed the pattern of God. Men continually reject Christ. This raises one question: what is darkness? I will answer this question now. God the father shut the door to darkness and destruction before Adam was born. Lust for the forbidden fruit released forces that God never wanted Adam to know about. This means that God would need another Adam. The second and last Adam is Jesus Christ. He is the sacrifice that brings all humanity back to God.

Genesis 1:1–5 tells the story of the Creation. He separated darkness and light. Father God said, "It is good." Our Father is a Watchman. His Spirit runs the neighborhood. He needed a human body. His presence is coming down. This Father is happy. He wants to live in the ground. Who is the ground? Is it a man? Who is the ground? Who is the head? Hold on until next time. We will talk about the ground. For now, lets talk about darkness. What is this darkness about?

The Hebrew word for darkness is *choshek* (kho-shek), *Strong's* reference number 2822. It refers to darkness, as well as misery or destruction and death. (Other words used in this definition are ignorance, sorrow, wickedness, night, and obscurity.) *Destruction* means "demolition." It also means slaughter. These spirits were in the atmosphere. They were waiting to commit manslaughter. Look at the word *misery*, great suffering because of pain. Wretchedness and sorrow is a part of misery. Poverty is included in this name.

What about the word *death*? You should know who that is. These spirits were waiting in the atmosphere. Who else is waiting to get in? Ignorance and sorrow are waiting. Ignorance wanted the human mind. Sorrow is right in the midst of it. This is mental suffering that afflicts the mind. At last you have wickedness and obscurity. Wickedness means morally bad. It is a spirit that will not submit to God. Wickedness could only make one sad. Obscurity means to be dim. It also means lacking light. These spirits are happy in the dark. They are also looking for a fight.

Almighty God ended this battle. His kingdom would never know war. Like a father looking out for His children, this Father shut the door. His Spirit dominated the airways. His spoken Word is a powerful light. His Spirit will control the globe. To God, this is not a fight.

I am sure these demons were screaming. They were very determined to win. God is the ultimate Ruler. Mankind was never to know sin.

God saw the face in the deep. He is ready to speak to the ground. A voice with a body is in it. God's treasure is in the ground. The ground is not a graveyard. Nobody will be a slave. Abuse and racism will not exist. None of the animals will need a cage. This is the first day of Creation. God divided darkness from light. His kingdom will never meet these spirits. God will simply call darkness night. To be continued!

As you know, Adam and Eve sinned. This gave darkness an opportunity to operate through people. God's image (Adam) is unclean, confused, and selfish. The Father no longer has a watchman. This means God needs a sacrifice. This sacrifice will be judged for the sins that all men committed. The sacrifice will demonstrate true submission. He would show man how to respect and love his Father. He shows man how desperately a son needs God.

He shows the warfare that a man encounters when his bride falls into lust. His life is destroyed and he is forced to trust his father. It drives him to God and he surrenders all. This sacrifice is Jesus Christ.

This is the beginning of divine government. The Sacrifice—Jesus—continues to submit to his Father. He demonstrates the love a man should have for his bride. He does that by giving himself to God completely. He receives the Spirit of his Father—God—and covers the bride. Then he asks the Father to make him one with her. The bride prepares to become one with Him. This happens because the Son knows what the Father wanted from the beginning. This raises two questions: Who is the bride? What does Jesus mean when He said, "Father, make them one as You and I are one"?

God gave us Christ. How is He connected to the tree? Where were all mankind in Genesis? Who is the face in the deep? The face in the ground is Adam. He is the first man. This face belongs to God. The flesh needs God's Spirit to rule the land.

Sin entered the human race. This caused God to ask for the tithes. He was going after the heart of the family. We have lived in lust and told lies. The roaring lion has entered the nations. He is in his final stage. I asked, "How much are you willing to give now?" I also asked you about the grave.

Men and women have lived in lust. They sleep around and will not give money. Your money is not what God really wanted. In the beginning, God gave man money. God brought money down. He is the Father who gave Adam everything. There was not one graveyard around.

In the entire first chapter of Genesis, you will see the word *good* written many times. Each day, God created something. At the end of each day, God said it was good. God continued to speak until all things were completed. On the seventh day, God rested according to Genesis 2:1–3. The body of man is God's resting place. God's Spirit will operate in the man.

*There's a Lion in the House and He Must Go!*

The Hebrew word for good is *towb* (tobe). It makes reference to a good man or woman, goods, pleasure, prosperity, and wealth. The *Strong's* reference number for good is 2896. God released wealth in the nation. He created the heavens and earth with the family in mind. Adam is given dominion over all things. Prosperity and riches are included. Adam is put in a wealthy place. God gave him a wife. She is the good thing that he did not have to find. God brought the woman to him. Adam proved to be trustworthy. He was qualified and prepared for a wife. He was already tested and groomed by his Father. Adam is released to love and be loved because he is obedient.

As you know, the first family became greedy. Lust released the father of lies. The serpent spirit will rule the nation. The house he will divide. The church and the government are separated. Division will run through the land. In the beginning the two are one—the church, and the government. Their own hands destroyed them. This raises two questions: What happened on 9/11? And, what will God do if He can get one woman to give a man both of her hands and give away a pair of her shoes? I will answer these questions now. The first reveals that the mass killing that took place on 9/11 were the result of the spirit of Jezebel in the airways. The second answer reveals the storm of one woman and her husband. The only thing God wanted from her is a face. Read on as I reveal the turning of the globe because one woman has built God an altar.

In the first chapter, I talked about the young lion. This

was according to Psalm 91:13. I told you the male lion has a mane. The female does not. This is how you can tell them a part. I told you that a village is surrounded by walls. The word *village* deals with a group of houses knitted together. It also defined as a community incorporated as a municipality. This means the community is combined into one body. They are organized as a legal corporation. The residents who live there have their own incorporated government. Their local affairs are handled according to there own beliefs.

This is the spirit that entered when the first family sinned. The walls of cement went up immediately. God was locked out. The human heart became very hard. The serpent spirit claimed the first house. Adam and Eve gave the unclean spirit its first village.

The fatherhood of God is locked out of the nation. The Pharaohs, Philistines, and Pharisees were already on the rise. The Pharaohs are those with a hard heart. The Philistines are those who put the glory of God in a room with another God, Dagon. The Pharisees are those who tempt the anointing instead of being corrected by it. They were the men who came to Jesus so that they could get a divorce. Nevertheless, Jesus did not release them. He showed them that they were not right with Him.

The same disorder continues today. All of these things are a part of the young lion. I told you the definition for *the young lion* comes from another Hebrew word. This definition will reveal that the walls were made of cement and asphalt. The definition refers to covering with bitumen. This will reveal the cruelness of the flesh. It kills, assassinates, and destroys other human lives when God is locked out. We build houses and buildings that will crush us because God is not in that building or in our homes.

The Hebrew word for young lion is *kephiyr* (kef-eer). This Hebrew word comes from the word *kaphar* (kaw-far), a primitive root. It means to cover (specifically with bitumen). Figuratively it means to expiate or condone. The *Strong's* reference number for kaphar (kaw-far) is 3722. The word *bitumen* describes asphalt found in its natural state. It is a hard material with a tar like residue. A mixture of this with sand or gravel is used for cementing, paving, or roofing. Mankind has locked God out as if they are covered in by strong walls. This was the beginning of bitumen. Their walls have been like asphalt.

This wall is a picture of how hard the human heart is. It wants nothing to do with God or His order. The young lion entered the nation. No one is aware of it. Throughout the Old Testament, this spirit has raged. In the New Testament, it continued. Today, it is fully developed. His mass killings have begun. This is the beginning of sorrows. On 9/11, the walls fell. The two towers were attacked. Many fathers died. Many men and women were covered with bitumen, or asphalt. This is a picture of what the flesh can do to another human being. The human heart is cruel and hard. It has become broken and angry. This goes back to the Garden of Eden. Now, humanity is ignoring God's Christ.

The word *expiate* means to suffer. Another word used to define *expiate* is *compensate*, which refers to making better or to make amends for wrongdoing. This is mind-boggling. How can this word be connected to the young lion? Only Jesus can make amends for mankind. He alone can remove our faults. He did that when He went to the cross. The penalty was paid. Jesus died a horrible death. This was done to set all men free.

Jesus died to save all sinners. All things were finished at the cross. This was an act of faith. Man must now choose life. We must receive God's Son Christ Jesus. He will give us knowledge of the Word. This will make us a strong weapon against the beast. It will empower us to resist the enemy's temptations to sin for his use.

Satan has a terrible way of making amends. I call it getting even. He cannot separate the wheat (godly) from the chaff (ungodly). His goal is to kill everyone. This would cause innocent people to die horrible deaths. Satan's way of improving anything is to throw out everything. To him, that is what you call purging and cleansing. We are devastated because we do not understand how we have helped the devil through disobedience. The human flesh is undisciplined and angry.

This is what happened on 9/11. Did you notice the serpent was coming after the very gate of our home base? He wants to destroy our government. This is a picture of a woman who is being strangled by the serpent spirit. It is a picture of a woman who has everyone's children, but there is no father for them. It is a picture of a woman who does not have a man of God to cover her. She is a woman who is constantly attacked and is always losing her man. She is a woman who no longer honors God and despises the very mention of His name. Most of all she has a lot of souls in her building. It is the enemy's desire to kill everyone in her house. It is the enemy's desire to kill the nations that she is responsible for. She is a picture of what men and women have done and are doing to each other. She needs prayer and must receive the mind of Christ.

Everything has climbed in and out of her gates. She is a woman who has been assaulted repeatedly. She is a picture of what happens to a woman when there is not a man of God in the house. Most of all, it is a picture of what the serpent does to a woman because she ignores her husband and God.

All of these things go back to the Garden of Eden. Satan entered the gates of the home. Adam never spoke out. He was totally dishonored. His wife was deceived. It continues today. The open gates must be shut. God is calling for His government. He loves her. The globe will go into travail for her. God is also calling for husbands and wives. Men and women must give up adultery and stop fornicating. Once again I hear God saying, "Sound the alarm!" This raises one question: Why did Prophetess Juanita Bynum do *No More Sheets*? I will answer this question now. She is the woman who gave away both of her hands in marriage, and a pair of her shoes. This will also answer another question I asked, Who will God use to call the globe unto repentance? God will use him to minister healing to every face. Read on as I reveal to you what God showed me in 2008.

Prophetess Juanita Bynum did *No More Sheets* around 1997. When I saw the tape for the first time, God began to deal with me in a heavy way. I do not know what people saw. I can only tell you that I saw the power of the Resurrection at work. God told me to watch her life. The course of her life would be the beginning of the globe turning. This raises two questions: Why did she do *No More Sheets*? And, what was going on in the atmosphere?

God told me Prophetess Bynum is a picture of the broken government. She is a picture of every single woman fighting against the serpent spirit that lives in the atmosphere. This serpent spirit lives inside many men and women. They are sleeping with whomever they want. God's authority has been abused. The image of God in the ground has become a graveyard. The image in the ground used to be the face of man. He would allow her to sing about His face. This raises more questions: Why did Prophetess Juanita Bynum give both of her hands to Bishop Weeks in their marriage ceremony? And from that question, I also ask, What was it that was changing in the spirit realm?

God told me, "I am calling the bride to build her house. She will prepare a place for me." God was telling me about mankind, His church, and I believed He was describing Prophetess Bynum, too.

The church no longer is pregnant with the fruit of

*There's a Lion in the House and He Must Go!*

the ground. She is giving birth to the great kings of the earth. God told me He was sending her to the kingdom that Adam gave away. It is divided. Men and women are filled with lust. Marriages are not honored. The body of Christ is His temple. God forbade man to use a woman and abuse the womb.

God then told me that many men are using women. This forced women to use men. The women are left uncovered and the children are hungry. The family is uncovered and without a priest, a man of God heading the household. They are left crying for God to feed them. They will be forced to wait until He can find someone to bless them.

Then, God asked me a question about Bynum, "Why did she give away a pair of her shoes?" Then He responded, "I am using her to kill the spirit of Jezebel that lives in the globe." God told me that He was specifically using Prophetess Bynum to kill the Jezebel spirit. This spirit entered when the first family sinned. The first woman fell into lust. Adam agreed with it. From that day, Adam has not had a voice. The family has been in trouble. Then He told me, "She [the church] has built me an altar." This raises one question: What did God mean when He said *altar*?

Reading Psalm 127:3 will help explain this next word the Lord gave me and that I now share. God said, "The human body is my temple. The only thing I wanted from the first woman is an image. She allowed it to die. She fell into lust. The human body became a graveyard. The fruit of the womb is my reward. The forbidden fruit represents my reward."

God revealed to me about Bynum's marriage, saying, "I placed Juanita with Thomas. I want her with a man of God who would say, 'Teach me how to love You.' This man has the heart of a father. He understands what the forbidden fruit means to Me. I have chosen her to bring down Babylon. She cannot do it by herself."

God said to me, "My Spirit has been left in a box. Men and women have killed my fatherhood. There is a place in the atmosphere that has been vacant since the fall of Adam. I just need one woman that wants to see My face. This is the picture of the true church. The human body is my temple. I have placed her [the church] with someone who is willing to redefine humanity's definition for love. Man is my face. Man is the image of God."

Then God asked me another question, "Why did the two of them [Bynum and Weeks] have a ministry called Global Destiny?" Here is God's response, "I have called them to the globe. The globe has not reached her destiny. It has been claimed by Babylon." Then, yet another question came, "Why did both have a ministry entitled, 'Teach me how to love You'? What does that have to do with the first family?" God then answered His question to me, saying, "The first two houses were destroyed. The altar of fatherhood was torn down. Lust and greed destroyed the first family. I have chosen Thomas and Juanita. She has built Me an altar. Every time she sat on the altar, I saw My face. Every time she was on the altar,

I saw a sweet smelling sacrifice." Then another question came, "What is going on in the atmosphere, and is it too much for two people to carry?" Again, He answered His own question to me and said, "Satan has claimed My princes, My men. They are born with the spirit of Cain. Some will grow up angry and fatherless. Their spirit will dominate the airways. Men will use women. Some will not know Me at all. The ground will keep its mouth open. I need one man to shut down the graveyard. The graveyard is not just the ground. It is the image of man. They have eaten the forbidden fruit. Graveyards are everywhere," God told me.

Earlier, I asked a question. I am sure by now you should know that there is another face in the ground. It is Babylon, with a mouth full of bones.

As I prepare to close out this chapter, I will give you another vision God gave me. This was in October of 2007. God showed me a vision of Bishop Weeks and the prophetess. It was in an open vision. I was wide awake. I saw Bishop Weeks. He was in the water. His hair looked jet black. His beard was full, not bushy at all. It was just nicely trimmed, yet full and very black. I saw him come out of the water. When he came out, he had his right hand up. It was all so fast. I did not see what was in his right hand. As I continued to look, I saw Juanita in his right hand. She was dressed in pure white. The garment was beautiful and it was white. Right before my eyes, I watched him lift her up very high. Then he released her to fly. Before my eyes, she turned into a white dove. I watched her soar higher than I had ever seen. Then I saw her go beyond the clouds.

My days and nights are filled with visions. They are the visions of eternity. I am always awake when God shows them to me. Then, early one morning, I woke up. This was around October of 2007. It was consistent. I heard Juanita's voice. She was singing. I could hear it as though I were in a place with her. Yet, it was coming from above. I also heard the voice of the bishop. He was singing. I wrote down some of the songs. They were songs that I had not heard before. Others were very intimate. This takes me back to another vision I had, one of the first.

I saw Bishop Weeks kneeling down in front of the prophetess. She was standing in front of him, dressed in white. His hands were stretched out as though his body formed a cross. His head was tilted back with his mouth wide opened. I watched Bynum take one of the biggest swords I have ever seen. She gently put it down his throat. Her hand was steady. Her face was focused. She did not thrust or force it. I watched him digest this sword, which was the length of his body while he was kneeling. He consumed the blade completely. The only thing that was left out of his mouth was the handle. I looked as the handle of the sword remained in her hands.

*There's a Lion in the House and He Must Go!*

This brings me to the next questions I have. Earlier, I asked, "Is there any man out there who is willing to say, 'Teach me how to love You'?" The answer to that question is yes! I also asked, "Who will God use to call the globe unto repentance?" This person is chosen. God will use him to minister healing to every face. Who is this man? This man is Bishop Thomas Weeks. God said, "No longer do I call you bishop. I call you apostle, prophet, pastor, teacher, and evangelist. You now enter into the place where Adam lived."

Adam was alone. His mind was drawn toward eternity. Adam knew that the forbidden fruit belonged to God.

As I write this concluding section of my book, the date is June 20, 2008. The time is around 6:30 a.m. My husband is out of town. The television is already on. As I flip through the channels, I have stopped at Fox Five. It was announced that the divorce of the Bishop and the Prophetess would be finalized. I believe this brings everyone to ground zero—and it will allow me to speak prophetically to the globe.

God had told me in one of my visions that Thomas and Juanita represent a new season. As I mentioned, today is June 20, 2008. It is the day before the first day of summer. At this time, the two are separated. The divorce is already being finalized. I have another vision and hear another word from God, as He tells me, "I am coming after the will of humanity. I will visit every house. I, God, have entered the globe. The will of a man is tied up in the forbidden fruit. In order for him to produce the right female image, he must guard the altar of his womb. In order for a woman to be covered, she must build Me an altar. Juanita built Me an altar."

The forbidden fruit belongs to God. It is not money God wanted in the beginning. He just wanted a family and a man of God.

I say to my spiritual mother, Juanita, the prophetess, "I caught the vision. You have always talked about loving the lamb. I have been sitting at home since the end of 2003. It is now 2008. Your love and wisdom lives in me."

To Bishop Weeks, I call you my spiritual father. God spoke to me in the beginning of 2005. He told me that you would be a father to me. He showed me the love you have for my mother, the prophetess. He also showed me your eagerness to assist her.

This brings me to a couple of questions: What is a man's assignment from God when it comes to the

*There's a Lion in the House and He Must Go!*

calling of his wife? What is a Proverbs 31 woman? I will answer both questions now. Then I will be getting close to closing out this book.

The first answer will reveal Adam's responsibility to name the woman. Then he must tell her what her assignment is. It has been revealed to him by God. It was settled in eternity before she came out of his image.

The second answer reveals God's need of a woman. She is a Proverbs 31 woman. God is calling every female to be one. The first woman became greedy. She was deceived and misguided. This woman was not lead. The serpent seduced her as a result of her own cravings. This is the beginning of lust. It would release a broken government. She destroyed her house. Adam was standing right there when it happened. It has left women and this government in disorder. Many men have become weakened and angry. They are feeling dishonored and have fallen into lust.

Genesis 3:20 says, "And Adam called his wife's name Eve; because she was the mother of all living." The Hebrew word for Eve is *Chavvah* (khav-vaw) and it means life giver Chavvah (or Eve), the first woman. The *Strong's* reference number for Eve 2332. God's government came out of Adam. She, the government, is called to give life. She will never kill her babies. Her prince will never have to fight. They desperately need each other. Both of them have God. She must submit as he teaches her. The beast wanted the man of God.

The beast is the serpent. He needs the consent of the

man. He wants to pull the government into lust. She is being covered by the man. The beast knew her assignment. So did the man of God. The beast came to mislead her. He wanted to break the pattern of God. He knew the power of the government. She is responsible for all. This woman is wealthy. Both of them are called. They must work together. God did not want them to fall. Disorder entered in. The Proverbs 31 woman must answer the call.

Being a Proverbs 31 woman is not easy. She has a great call. I will give you the Hebrew word. Her order is very tall. I will only give one word. This woman must fight. Get ready, every woman. You are being provoked to fight.

Proverbs 31:10 says, "Who can find a virtuous woman? for her price is far above rubies." The Hebrew word for virtuous is *Chayil* ( khah-yil ), *Strong's* reference number 2428. (It means a force, whether of men, or other resources. It also means army, wealth, and strength.) The virtuous woman is filled with strength. In the beginning, it (her strength) came from the man. Eve is a powerful woman. Her image came from the man. They were supposed to help each other. They allowed darkness to come down. The woman became lustful. Darkness was ready to attack the ground.

The ground is their beginning. It is a picture of the man. God did not want a graveyard. God created a man. The first woman became selfish. Darkness would soon come down. The firmament will eventually break. Then the waters will return to the ground.

In the beginning, the waters had a face. God has set their course. He separated the waters from the waters. Lust took them off their course. Sin broke down the firmament. That is why the waters are coming down. What is this water, anyway? How is it connected to the ground?

Let's continue with the Proverbs 31 woman. I will dig deeper into the Hebrew definition for *virtuous*. This word will give the details of everything the first woman possessed. She is a woman of power and force. God expected her to tread on the serpent with Adam's assistance. She has a military background. This is one that can give birth to an army for God. The only thing she needed was Adam's instructions. This means any other voice is the voice of disorder. She is obligated to her house first. If she listens to any other voice, she is in lust.

Recall the definition for the word *virtuous* I gave earlier. The virtuous woman is declared to be a woman of force. She is an army. This woman has wealth. These are the only three terms I will comment on: *force*, *army*, and *wealth*.

In the beginning, the woman came out of the man. She is strong only because she came out of God's image. She is kept only if she listens to the image. Her household will stand if she honors the image. Adam is the image that will protect what comes out of him. As you know, the first woman fell. Her husband never corrected her. I continue to say to the men, "Speak up!" Only speak what God said. Please do not argue. Go to God if she will not listen. He is turning our human hearts back toward Him. This means we cannot eat the forbidden fruit.

Now let's look at the Proverbs 31 woman again. I will show you what God expects of her. She is a woman who must fight for the image God lost. Her strength is for her household first. She is a woman who does business. This woman keeps her husband from spoiling. She wins his heart and his trust. She understands her first assignment is her house.

Again, recalling the word *virtuous*, the definition includes the word *force*. Proverbs 31:10 asks, "Who can find a virtuous woman?" And I ask, who can find a woman of force? That is, who can find a woman who has power to act effectively and vigorously? To act effectively means to hit your target. To act vigorously means that a person is living and growing with full vital strength. They are prepared for battle. This woman is ready to fight. Her warfare is to come against anything that wants her house. The question is asked, "Who can find a virtuous woman?" And again I say, who can find a woman who will fight for her house?

The next word from the definition of the term *virtuous* is *army*. When seeking a virtuous woman, who can find a woman with a military background in God? Who can find a woman who can organize a body of soldiers, and then prepares them to fight for God? Her strategy will destroy the warfare in the atmosphere. The anointing in her will provoke resurrection power to come into the universe. This anointing will hit the Babylonian image in the ground. When this happens, men will have no need to spoil.

The ground is a picture of man and everything that came out of him. In the beginning, the ground did not look like a graveyard. This raises one question: what does it mean to spoil? I will now continue with the last word about the virtuous woman.

The last word is *wealth*. Once again, I quote Proverbs 31:10 and ask, "Who can find a virtuous woman?" Who can find a woman of wealth? Who can find a woman who has everything, yet recognizes her need to be covered by one man that loves God? Who can find a virtuous woman who will listen to her husband instead of the voice of the serpent? Who can find a virtuous woman who has everything, yet still God can use her to stop her husband from spoiling? Who can find a virtuous woman who will not spoil what God wants for her and the man she is married to? Who?

In the beginning, the first woman was virtuous. She was the virtuous woman the first man did not have to find. She was a woman of force, but made the wrong choice. She acted effectively and vigorously, but aimed at the wrong target. She grew in strength, but her choice was an attack against her husband. Both of them were supposed to help each other, but failed to do so. They were supposed to be fruitful and multiply, but fell into lust. So once more I ask, "Who can find a virtuous woman?" (Prov. 31:10).

The first woman had a military background. She and her husband, Adam, were supposed to produce more princes for God. Greed gave the army of princes to the spirit of Babylon. Men would be born with hard hearts. Adam named his wife after she sinned. He never corrected her in love. This is the beginning of lust and anger.

The spirits will dominate the atmosphere. They will live inside the princes that Adam gave away. The spirit of lust manifested in Adam and his wife. The spirit of anger manifested in their ministry, their children.

This is when Cain kills his brother Abel. Two sons came out of the same house. Two parents divided God's government. The serpent nature entered the human body. Lust destroyed the governmental order of God. The ground opened its mouth. In the natural realm, it looks like the ground. In the spirit realm, it was the mouth of Adam. His lust destroyed his house. It happened because of his wife. He went along with it. Today, the mouth of the ground is still open. Men and women are dying prematurely. The human body has been abused and misused. The fatherhood of God died in the garden. They did not know what the forbidden fruit represented.

Who can find a woman who wants to be covered by one man? Who can find a woman who understands that God gives you one man in order to keep the serpent spirit off of you? Who can find a woman who understands that

*There's a Lion in the House and He Must Go!*

she can fall into lust without a man's assistance? Who can find a woman who's willing to be loved and corrected? Who can find this virtuous, wealthy woman?

The first woman was wealthy because she was connected to God's image. She and her husband were wealthy because God is their Father. God never intended for two people to be blessed, but then go their separate ways. He expected the family to grow up in one house. God wanted one nation. Lust destroyed the house. Greed caused disagreements.

Men and women gladly got married. They soon divorced. Many would not know that eating the forbidden fruit is the root cause of divorce. It hardens the heart. Then, it divides the government and the church and produces a society that hates God and has no respect for human lives.

This is the spirit of Jezebel. It flourishes in a no-name society that does whatever it wants. It is a society that despises parenthood. It is a picture of a woman who has been left uncovered. She dies because she refuses to submit. She is dead because no one corrected her. God judges her because her husband agreed with her. He is the voice that is supposed to correct her. Even Jezebel's husband watched her operate in disorder. Once again, this goes back to the first woman.

In 2 Kings, Jezebel died. She is mentioned again in the Book of Revelation, yet her spirit lives. The first woman caused her husband to spoil. Her greed was the beginning of the Jezebel spirit. Her husband's agreement with

131

it left God without a voice. Their power of agreement locked God out of the nation. Read on as I reveal this truth. This is what happens when Jezebel gets in the water.

In Genesis 2:10, it says, "And a river went out of Eden to water the garden; and from thence it was parted, and became into four heads." The Hebrew word for river is *nahar* (naw-hawr), *Strong's* reference number 5104. This word means a stream, and includes the sea, the Nile and Euphrates rivers. The words prosperity and flood are used figuratively. God wanted the land to prosper. He also needed Adam's blood. Adam is created in God's image. He is born without sin. God did not want him to know evil. He did not want darkness to get in. The river went into four heads. The river came out of Adam's home. Did you know Adam lived in Eden? Do you think God wanted dry bones? (God is a spirit.) He came into agreement with the blood. The blood could not become contaminated. If it did, there would be a flood.

The Hebrew word for heads is *Ro'sh* (roshe). It is from an unused root meaning to shake, the head as the part most easily shaken. Whether literally or figuratively, it makes reference to the word beginning a captain, chief, and high priest. The word *poor* is also in this definition. The *Strong's* reference number for heads is 7218. A river went out of Eden. From that point, it formed four heads. It first made a stop by the garden. Then it continued to be led. Did you notice it means "to shake"? It even says shake the head. The head is the part that is easily shaken. God wanted the river to be led. Did you notice

*There's a Lion in the House and He Must Go!*

the word *beginning*? The river came out of the home. What about the word *captain*? This river is not alone. The word *captain* means chief or leader. It would never get out of control. *River* has many definitions. The half has not been told. At last, the word *river* means "first." It also mentioned "poor." High priest is written in the definition. Tell me, who is waiting at the door? God set the course of the river. God included the river in the plan. The river and the waters are connected together. Both—river and waters—will attack if God loses His man.

In 2 Kings 9:30, it says, "And when Jehu was come to Jezreel, Jezebel heard of it; and she painted her face, and tired her head, and looked out at a window." This is a Scripture passage about Jezebel. At this time, she is already born. I will use the Hebrew word for *head*. I will show you where her spirit came from. I will compare her head to the rivers' heads. Both of them will be the same. This is what happens when Jezebel gets in the house. The kingdom will never be the same.

As I already have quoted a few times, Genesis 2:10 reads, "And a river went out of Eden to water the garden; and from thence it was parted, and became into four heads." And as I also earlier cited, the Hebrew word that applies to the rivers' heads and Jezebel's head is *Ro'sh* (roshe). A river went out of Eden, Adam's home. God made Adam the head. Notice the spirit of the high priest is in the river. Another spirit wanted to get in. The priestly man is in the house with the woman, Eve. He will protect the human bones. The two mindsets

133

must become one. There will never be a fight over the throne.

Earlier, I asked you a question. I asked, "Who is waiting at the door?" God did not want them to know this spirit. It snuck into Eden through the back door. This spirit wanted the woman. It also wanted the man. Darkness is waiting on the outside. These spirits needed both of them. Take notice of the definition. A shaking is going on. Who will be the head? Will the serpent sit on the thrown? Who will be the captain? Will the river drown the house? It is really up to the man. Will Jezebel get in the house?

Jezebel is a spirit. In the beginning, it did not have a body. Any body will do. This spirit needed two bodies. The woman, Eve, was deceived by the serpent. It must be corrected by the man, for if he fails, Babylon will enter. You will eventually know Jezebel as she is.

We have discussed her in the Old Testament. She has a shape and a form. Then we read about her death. What does she have to do with the whore? The whore is mentioned in Revelation. Jezebel is mentioned again. (Its' time to take up a wailing! Let's fight for women and men.)

God is our Father. He is not guilty of drowning the globe. What kind of Father will He be? Who is drowning so many souls? God is a Spirit. His Spirit lives in man. Man is placed in authority. May I paint a picture of the land?

Man came out of the ground. The ground is the first

womb. The womb had water everywhere. God created a body for the waters and the womb. The head came out first. The head is the face of a man. The man is the head of the body. This head is the covering for the land. The head released another body. It was woman, taken out of man. What will happen to the womb called the ground? What will the waters do when God loses his man?

The waters will come back together, like a pregnant woman giving birth. Death will manifest instead of life. Death will rule the earth. Like a thief passing through the night, the water will run from house to house. Like a mass killer on the loose, you do not know when he will strike.

Who in the world is this water? It has decided to drown the house. Stay tuned until next time. I warn you, Jezebel is in the house. Jezebel is a spirit. It entered in through Adam and Eve. God is calling the globe into order. She will reach her destiny!

Earlier, I asked, "What does it mean to spoil?" I will answer this question now. This will reveal the greed of the first woman. The lust she released continues today. Her choice began a process that leads to the death of her house and the entire globe. Her choice in the garden shows us what spirit she had respect for. The spirit they honored now rules the atmosphere. The serpent spirit operates in large empires and inside our homes. This serpent nature lives in people and has manifested in our children. They are angry, hungry, hopeless, and in need of help. As parents and adults, we have been cunning, proud, cruel, selfish, lustful, greedy, and deceived.

Throughout the Old Testament, we have seen the serpent spirit operating in women and men. It has continued in the New Testament because of lust and greed. Today, God is calling for lust and greed to die. The ground is evidence of what lust and greed does to men and women. It kills the entire family. There is nothing left except dead, dry bones. God's purpose is lost.

Now, in this hour, God is calling every woman to become a Proverbs 31 woman. You will become the woman that your husband desperately needs. He will become the man that stays inside of one house. No longer will the two of you fail to help each other. Read on and be blessed. God wants women to stop men from spoiling. Both of you are obligated to love and trust one another.

In Proverbs 31:10–11, it says, "Who can find a virtuous woman? for her price is far above rubies. The heart of her husband doth safely trust in her, so that he shall have no need of spoil." The Hebrew word for spoil is *shalal* (shaw-lawl). It means booty, prey, and spoil. *Strong's* reference number is 7998. When a man spoils, he becomes booty and prey for someone else. This means he is taken by force. Then he is treated like an animal. He then gets attacked and used by someone that does not value him. Those who take him by force do not know his value. Their purpose for seizing him is for their own selfish gain. Sometimes he is killed, so that someone else can have food on their table.

We have seen this animalistic behavior in the example of slavery. Using people of any race in forced labor is from the spirit of prostitution. We have seen this animalistic behavior in relationships. Men and women have used one another. We have seen this behavior in marriages. One person, if not both, has had an affair. What it all boils down to, is that men and women have used and hurt each other. All of these things are from the spirit of the lion. This is the behavior of an animal working through people. In the animal kingdom, they feed off of one another. They kill one another in order to survive. It does not matter who becomes their prey.

This type of behavior has trickled down through the centuries. Whenever a man falls into lust, the enemy claims everything that comes out of him. The human body becomes a house for whoredom. The human body is a gate that releases princes. The princes are male children. Some of these princes do not have their father's name. The nations of the world are a picture of a body that does not have a father or God. Lust in the garden did this to the globe.

This has caused many men to grow up without being trained and mentored by their fathers. They do not respect God because their father was not present. A father in the home is supposed to teach a son submission and obedience. Submitting to their father is designed to lead them back to God. This means a man is prepared to be in authority the right way. He is qualified to be in authority because he has been submissive, trained, and molded by his father.

Let's look at the entire scripture again. This will reveal the broken fellowship of man and God. He is without God because he has been disfigured by the female. She is left uncovered and therefore fell into lust. The serpent spirit rules because we do not see how we are helping that spirit. Our marriages are destroyed because we do not understand God's order in the physical realm. Here is the same Scripture passage. The Hebrew definition for heart will follow. Proverbs 31:10–11 says, "Who can find a virtuous woman? for her price is far above rubies. The heart of her husband doth safely trust in her, so that he shall have no need of spoil." The Hebrew word for heart is *Leb* (labe), from Strong's reference number 3820. God wants a man to feel safe with his wife. He wants the heart of the man to trust his own wife. Her choices will determine the outcome of her house. She has the power to stop him from spoiling.

The word *heart* is used very widely. The Proverbs 31 woman has a huge responsibility. She will affect the feelings, the will, and the intellect or mind of her husband. A wife has the ability to build up his courage, causing him to become courageous. Her actions can bring comfort to her house. At the same time, she can cause him to become broken and hard. This means that when the serpent spirit enters, lust is inevitable.

Once again, everything goes back to the forbidden

fruit. The first woman was deceived. Her choice was a direct attack against Adam's mind. His will to continue with God was broken. The human mind and his feelings were turned away from God. The woman who was supposed to help him attacked him. He willingly assisted her, which means they spoiled each other.

All of these things have brought us to the season we are now in. Ever since that time, the human heart has become hard and rigid. At the same time, it is trying to experience love and care for one spouse without being unfaithful. Once again, the globe must renew or update the definition for love.

I know at this time it looks like the woman has a large responsibility. However, I will take you to a New Testament scripture. This will reveal why Christ came. He judged sin so that man can receive his position back as the head. The man sets the tone for love by becoming a picture of Christ. He follows the example by giving himself completely to God. The woman respects him, which is designed to provoke the man to lay down his life for her. Both of them are a picture of the church and must help each other.

Christ is the Savior and empowers both of them to help each other. Every husband and wife must teach the other how to love each other. Warning! Do not be so quick to holler that you already know. Quote me! You don't!

Ephesians 5:21–24 says, "Submitting yourselves one to another in the fear of God. Wives, submit yourselves unto your own husbands, as unto the Lord. For the husband is the head of the wife, even as Christ is the head of the church: and he is the saviour of the body. Therefore as the church is subject unto Christ, so let the wives be to their own husbands in every thing." Spouses must help each other. You have the power to stop the lust. We must submit to one another. God does not want us to break up. Both must fear the Lord. The woman must recognize her head, the man.

As we look deeper into this Scripture passage, listen to what God said. He sets the kingdom back in order. Another Adam is on the scene. This Adam is obedient. He operates as a king. This king is God's example. He will lead the man of God. The mind of the king must get in the man. This is a picture of the church and the rod, Adam and Eve.

This brings us back to the beginning. All God wanted was a man. The man was supposed to cover the woman, the body of Christ in the church. The woman should cover the man. The man will protect the family. Both of them will work for God. The first family failed to do that. They failed to help one another in God.

Now God has given us Christ. Christ has become the Head. Christ is the man's Example. He shows a man how to be the head. You are called to cover your wife. You have been restored by God. You must use His Word as your guideline. Now, go forth and protect one another through Christ.

This is the divine order: one woman belongs to one

man, and both of them are a picture of Christ. The family is shaping each other again. The two parties are one body in Christ. Both of them belong to God.

Let's look at that passage from Ephesians again. I will show where the family has gone wrong. Ephesians 5:21–24 says, "Submitting yourselves one to another in the fear of God. Wives, submit yourselves unto your own husbands, as unto the Lord. For the husband is the head of the wife, even as Christ is the head of the church: and he is the saviour of the body. Therefore as the church is subject unto Christ, so let the wives be to their own husbands in every thing." Christ is the Savior of the body. He came to save us from ourselves.

The flesh can be lustful and greedy. Most of us think only of self. Greed and lust have destroyed men and women. The family has had no restraint. We have taken what belongs to God. This is why couples have begun to faint.

Husbands and wives do not submit to each other anymore. Some couples do not listen to God. In the beginning, man was God's image. This is how the family would hear from God. Many women are listening to the serpent's voice. Men are doing the same. The family is living in confusion.

In many places, Ephesians 5:21–24 is misquoted. What does the word *everything* mean to God? What would Christ ask His bride to do? The human body has become a grave. Earlier I made a comment. I told you Pharaoh did not mind reproduction, as long as you kill the male babies. I also asked what kind of spirit or people will be left if all the male babies were killed. Read on and be healed. God is setting order in the family and the globe. He wants women to see why they have suffered. He wants men to see why they are hurting. All creation is groaning and wants to know who the sons of God really are.

God expected the first man to cover and instruct the first woman. Lack of knowledge caused her to honor the serpent. This released the Pharaoh spirit into the globe. Her husband gave up his authority when he assisted her. The government is broken. This is the serpent of lust standing between two people. God is locked out of the globe and their house. Women would be left uncovered. They will become professional women who do not have time for marriage. Men would become important and successful at the same time. Both will make time for sex with anybody they feel like having it with. Having a marriage with children will become a total dishonor.

As we grow closer to the End Times, the atmosphere will become more corrupt. It will not stop until we understand that the firmament is broken and the heart of God must be healed. The heart of God is in the chest of all mankind. Men must become one with the female in their lives. This means we cannot eat the forbidden fruit. It also means that God is calling every man out of the bed with that woman who is successful and powerful, but she does not want to make the relationship legal.

The Proverbs 31 woman is a woman of force. This

means she is a woman who has power to act effectively and vigorously. She is prepared for battle. I talked about this earlier. Let's look back at this definition again. I am writing it again on purpose. This is designed to help men understand what happens when it looks like a woman of God falls short. It is also designed to show women how we are powerful and yet vulnerable when we do not allow our husbands to guide us with all that strength.

Disorder in the garden has caused all of us to use our power and authority to aim at what we wanted. That was fine when we were single. But it is horrible when you do not have God. Getting married brings a Proverbs 31 woman into using her anointing and authority for her house, first. Every woman can stand to have a class on how to be a wife, so put your fingers down and stop pointing. Let's look at the definition again. As we look I see God bringing healing to the entire globe. The Hebrew word for virtuous is *Chayil* ( khah-yil ), *Strong's* reference number 2428.

She is a woman of force because of men or other resources. This means women have become powerful through some source. You may have had assistance from a family friend. Maybe it was your father or mother. Perhaps it was your pastor. For some women, it was just you and God. This has produced deception in us. The enemy wants us to think we have gotten somewhere on our own. It is his goal to bring us back into the mindset that allowed sin to enter in for the first woman.

Disorder pulls us into lust. It keeps us listening to

temptations. It has caused us to ignore our husbands. Men have been guilty of misusing their authority. Now, many women are saying, "I don't need a man." At the same time, they have a different man in their beds every night. God is not pleased.

Many women are disappointed over how they grew up. Many were left without a father. There was not a man to submit to. There were a lot of men coming in and out of the house. They used our mothers and may have even tried to sleep with us. This has caused young girls to grow up arrogant, angry, and ruthless. They eventually became successful powerful women who do not value or respect men.

Once again, this goes back to the garden. Wanting power and disrespecting men is of the serpent spirit. This has caused men to disrespect women and have no respect for the womb. There are many women in this world who look like Proverbs 31 women. They are powerful and very successful. At the same time, they have chosen to remain single while sleeping around.

Disorder in the garden has caused the serpent to take on a human form. Now, men and women have the luxury of being powerful and ignoring God. Out of the blackness of our hearts, we have produced all kinds of evil. It is on the market for sale. Men and women have used each other. Once again I hear God saying, "Sound the alarm!"

In this hour, God is calling men and women back to the house. The house is the garden where they planted,

## There's a Lion in the House and He Must Go!

plucked up, or killed what was growing. It has not been easy for many men to recognize the value of the woman. How can they, when they may not have had a father themselves, who would have told them who they are or what they are worth? This has forced men and women to put one another down. A man cannot give something that was never given to him. This has left women angry and lustful.

Women have become prizes or gifts to men who do not know a woman's value. We are married and cannot express God's definition for love. Then we continue to produce children by someone we will not marry. This forces women to use somebody's husband or a single man because she has to feed the children. Some men were already married, but it did not stop him. Once again I hear God saying, "Sound the alarm!"

The first woman had great respect for the serpent. She proved that a woman can get into a mess without the help of anyone. The first man was not deceived. He proved that he could live alone and be disciplined. However, God said that it was not good for Adam to remain alone.

Man is required by God to cover and lead the female. God is calling for Adam. He sees him in his fig leaves. He loves him, and still calls him His man. This means God is expecting men to become humble and broken before Him. God is ready to set order in the globe.

We are in the Last Days. The church has had to fight for every household. Pastors and bishops have been stretched beyond their limits. Prophets and prophetesses have been pulled apart by hurting people. The kingdoms of this world have children everywhere. Many men will continue to dishonor marriage while single women continue to have babies. They will point their finger at the church, while the weight of disorder breaks us down. The kings of the earth have become slaves to lust. Great men and women of God are feeling the pressure of disorder because the atmosphere is completely corrupted.

God does not have a face because many men are doing what they want. Children are being born every second. These children are left for adoption or left in the foster system. Maybe their grandparents have taken them in. These are children that will grow up injured and incomplete. But maybe they will step between the walls of the church. Some pastor and his wife will become the parents that speak into their lives.

While pastors and their wives continue to preach, more people are being put in their presence. This disorder has robbed pastors, bishops, prophets, and prophetesses of quality time with their spouses. It has caused an explosion in the atmosphere and implosions in the waters, oceans, and seas. The kingdoms of this world have many children in them, but they do not have a king.

Today, mankind does not understand that Jesus is the King that restored all humanity back to God. Your body must become His temple so that Jesus can come alive in

*There's a Lion in the House and He Must Go!*

you. This will allow a man to become a king in his own house. He will use the Word of God as his guide.

Christ is the Savior of your body and household. When you fail to honor him, it forces you to run your house like a wild beast. Lust will cause you to become a weapon against your own house. Your flesh will cause you to treat your spouse like an enemy.

Earlier, I said I would give you some words of wisdom. Some of you have children by other people. You are now with someone else. Before I give the advice, I must share with you another vision God gave me about Bishop Weeks and Prophetess Juanita. Once again, I was not asleep. It was the morning of August 9, 2008. The time was 7:18 a.m. My clock is eleven minutes fast, which means that this vision began at approximately 7:07 a.m. I waited to write an ending to this book.

You probably noticed that I said I was getting close to closing this book several paragraphs ago. Well, now I close. Again, it was August 9, 2008. As I lay asleep, I heard an angelic voice. Who was it? Once again, my vision contained the singing voice of Prophetess Juanita Bynum. She was singing a song. As she sang the song, I listened. In each of these visions, she was singing in a place that is far beyond the clouds. Yet, I knew it was near me because I live in eternity, although my body is here. As she sang, Bishop Weeks began to sing with her. Their voices were in perfect harmony. The melody was so sweet. I will write what both of them sang. I will put their names by the verses they sang. As I listened, I knew how God wanted me to end this book. Here are the words that I heard them sing:

> (The Prophetess sang) You must remember me. You must remember me.
>
> (Bishop sang) You must let me through the gate!
>
> (The Prophetess sang) I know!
>
> (Bishop sang) You must remember me.
>
> (The Prophetess sang) You must remember my mind.
>
> (Both sang) You must remember me.
>
> (The Prophetess sang) You must remember me.
>
> (Both sang) You must remember me.

With this song came a revelation from God. It will reveal how the first woman is supposed to be a doorway for the princes that God wanted to be born. The first woman is also the one who would determine the outcome of Adam's destiny. She has power over unseen forces and does not know it. God has empowered her to be a pillar in the globe.

Her rib is connected to the sky. Together they are one body. The rib in her body came out of him. This makes her powerful only because she is covered by God's image. God never wanted a woman to fight the snake by herself. Adam is the face of God and must instruct and cover the woman. Read on as I explain and give you the Scripture passage and Hebrew word for the word *rib*.

Genesis 2:22–23 says, "And the rib, which the LORD God had taken from man, made he a woman, and brought her unto the man. And Adam said, This is now bone of my bones, and flesh of my flesh: she shall be called Woman, because she was taken out of Man." God is Spirit. His Spirit has entered the man. The human body belongs to God. He wants an army of women and men. His Spirit is reproducing. He will never go back to the ground. Adam's body belongs to God. Adam's body came from the ground. The ground has a shape and a form. It is a picture of man. God is in this human body. Inside the body is a woman. Reproduction must continue. God took one of the ribs. Out of Adam came the female. How important are the ribs? I will answer this now. Read on and be blessed.

The human ribs are very important. They have a connection to the sky. The bones will never become twisted. Nobody will ever die. The waters will never attack us. Darkness will never come down. God separated the waters from the waters. God's Spirit will cover the ground. Let's look at the definition for the word *rib*.

The Hebrew word for rib is *tsela* (tsay-law); or feminine tsal'ah (tsal-aw). It means a rib literally of the body or figuratively of a door; figuratively of an object or the sky; architecturally a timber or plank, especially floor or ceiling. The *Strong's* reference number for the word *ribs* is 6763. God is the master Architect. He built two mansions in the land. Both mansions are one in the Spirit. These mansions are a woman and a man. Both of them are doors for more princes. Unity will release one government in the land.

The Architect will continue to build. He will build more mansions in the land. This time, God will allow men to build buildings. God did not want trouble in the land. They could not eat the forbidden fruit. This would cause great destruction in the land. This raises several questions: did the first family eat the forbidden fruit? What happened in the Old Testament about the water once sin entered? What will happen in the Last Days because God's water does not have a face? Did the waters ever have a face? Where did darkness go once sin entered? I will answer these questions now. Then I will give my closing advice for those who have children and are married to someone other than the childrens' parents.

Yes, the first family ate the forbidden fruit. The atmosphere will soon break down. Everyone will be brought to ground zero. The waters will return to the ground. Darkness will enter in. We will see the first flood. Noah built an ark. Need I say any more?

At last, the waters will divide. We have already seen it once. Pharaoh's army was drowned. God is looking for His face again. The government is completely corrupt.

The firmament continually pounds. God will give His Son. His Son will speak to the ground.

A woman is caught in adultery. Men want to stone her to death. Jesus would not allow them. He came to rule over death. Then He spoke to the ground. The ground is a picture of man. He stooped down and wrote with His finger. Jesus is speaking to dead men.

Who is this adulterous woman? This woman represents the church. She is a woman left uncovered. She is in adultery and she is hurt. She is a picture of every woman. She is a picture of the globe. Men and women have hurt each other. The half has not been told. This woman is in adultery. How is adultery defined by God? How did adultery enter in? What does adultery have to do with robbing God?

In the Last Days, the waters will attack. Every man must build an ark. This ark is not a big boat. I am talking about letting God in your heart. His fatherhood wants to live in you. The globe belongs to God. The waters are out of control. This is what they are doing now.

The waters are running from house to house. This water is connected to man. It is also connected to his house. What is going on with the waters and man? It will creep in through the basement. We would simply call it a flood. It shows up uninvited. For years it did not kill anyone. Through the basement sewer it entered. You can expect it during a storm. Then it will leave without warning. The waters did not say a thing to anyone. Like death looking for the blood, the waters passed over your house. For a long time they did not do damage, but when they left, you still had a house.

Once again the sun would shine. You did not think about it twice. The storm just passed over. To all of us it was nice. Then again, it would thunder and lightning. Once again we would see the flood. Eventually it became angry. Yet it did not kill anyone. Once again, it crawled in through the sewer; through the basement it entered in. Each time the water got higher, unannounced it showed up again. What can make this water so angry? Why is this water out of control? This water needs two bellies. May I give you a little bit more?

In the beginning, God set up the firmament. He separated the waters from the waters. Before He separated them, He saw His image. God's face is seen in the waters. Darkness is upon the face. The Spirit of God is moving, too. God spoke light into the waters. What is God preparing to do?

The waters are with God in heaven. The waters are connected to man. He put a firmament between the waters. On the sixth day, He made man. The man is God's image. God's Spirit will live in the man. Let me show you what is happening now. History is repeating itself.

This water does not have a belly. That is why it is causing a flood. In the beginning, God had two bellies. They were responsible for the waters above. This is not just natural water. It is very much alive. That is why God separated the waters. These waters are part of the bride,

*There's a Lion in the House and He Must Go!*

Adam and the woman, and all humanity. God needed Adam and the woman. He needed their bellies for the waters. They became lustful and greedy. The Jezebel spirit entered the water. Nobody would understand it. Then the waters were given to Christ. Who is this water, anyway? How are the waters connected to Christ?

This water is out of control. The atmosphere is shaking. Heaven has too much water to hold. This water has become desperate. It is fighting to stay alive. This water goes back to the garden. Adam let the waters die.

In the beginning, the waters had a face. The waters are connected to man. God separated the waters. Then God looked at the dry land. God continued to speak. On the sixth day, he made a man. Now, water is above and below. The waters will not be brought together again.

On the seventh day, God rested. His Spirit is in the house. The fatherhood of God is in man. The body of man is God's house. A river went out of Eden. God did not want a flood. He wanted the land to prosper. He needed Adam's blood. The water and the blood agreed, God would rule the house. He will rule through the man. The woman will protect the house. The house is the male body. The waters are ready to flow. The woman will determine the outcome. Which way will the waters go?

As you know, the first family sinned. The woman shut the door. Adam supported her. May I give you a little more? The human bones are now twisted. They are crippled and lame. The bones are being crushed. God is not to blame. Look into the airways. Who are the stars? They represent men. They have been claimed by Babylon. Remember the ribs? (They are connected to the sky.) God is looking for His face. Where is His face now?

This brings me back to my vision. The waters have a face. Juanita Bynum built God an altar. God, please show me Your face. Man is God's image. God is calling for all. Why did I see them in the water? What is this water about? I will show you the beginning. I will give you a peek. (Love starts in the spirit.) Let's talk about sheets. God is the Father. His Spirit is coming down. He needed a body. This body needs a crown. The waters are important. This water is alive. Man is God's body. I will not talk about the crown. This is the pattern. There would never be a flood. God wants the land to prosper. He needed Adam's blood. As you know, Adam sinned. This broke the firmament down. This is how it looked before sin entered. God brought heaven down.

Genesis 1:1–5 reads, "In the beginning God created the heaven and the earth. And the earth was without form, and void; and darkness was upon the face of the deep. And the Spirit of God moved upon the face of the waters. And God said, Let there be light: and there was light. And God saw the light, that it was good: and God divided the light from the darkness. And God called the light Day, and the darkness he called Night. And the evening and the morning were the first day." This is the first day. God's Spirit is in control. Adam has not been born. Heaven will unfold. Darkness is present. So is the light. One face is in the waters. There will never be a fight. The face is God's image. It is the first man of God. His body must be formed. His body belongs to God. The body is in the ground. It is beneath all of the waters. Like a baby waiting to be born, the face is seen in the waters.

God has a process. This is the first stage. (Love starts in the spirit.) The ground is not a grave. Let's see how God did it. He wanted a bride. The father started with a man. Inside the man is the bride. This is the first day of the Creation. On the seventh day, He finished the plan. God separated the light from darkness. God's Spirit will live in the man. This raises one question: what did God do with the waters as He prepared to live in the ground? I will answer this question now. Read on and be blessed.

A pounding is in the atmosphere. What could this be? It is not a category four storm waiting to kill me. This pounding is passion. God is in love. Passion is in the atmosphere. How does God spell love? "Teach me how to love You." I do not want to be alone. Adam will be born. He will feel alone. God is his Father. His body belongs to God. Adam is not born yet. It is just the globe and the Spirit of God.

I will give you the second day. God's Spirit continually moves. His Spirit dominates the airways. Darkness cannot rule. I am revealing God's pattern. Heaven and earth have agreed. Love will wait in the firmament. A pounding heart will beat. God is the Father. His Spirit is coming down. Adam and Eve must define love. God's Spirit is one with the ground.

This raises one question: how do we know for sure that there is pounding taking place in the atmosphere? I will answer this question now. I will do that by giving you the second day of the Creation. God called the firmament heaven. He sat the firmament in the midst of the waters. This becomes a picture of heaven standing between the waters that God separated. This means water will remain below. The waters below are called the sea. Water will also be above. This water is connected to humanity. God never wanted the firmament to break. The waters would not attack the ground. The waters above just needed two bellies. They will follow the face in the ground.

Genesis 1:6–8 tells us, "And God said, Let there be a firmament in the midst of the waters, and let it divide the waters from the waters. And God made the firmament, and divided the waters which were under the firmament from the waters which were above the firmament: and it was so. And God called the firmament Heaven. And the evening and the morning were the second day." This is the second day.

I will give you the Hebrew word for firmament. It includes the word *expanse*, which I will discuss later. The firmament was pounding. Love waited to come down. Passion is saying, "I do not want lust. I need a body to work through in the ground."

The Hebrew word for firmament is *Raqiya* (Raw-kee'-ah), *Strong's* reference number 7549. (It means expanse which is the unbroken surface of the sky.) The word

### There's a Lion in the House and He Must Go!

*Raqiya* comes from the Hebrew word *Raqa* (raw-kah), and refers to pounding the earth. It is *Strong's* reference number 7554.

On the second day, the earth began to pound. This is a sign of passion. God wants to live in the ground. He separated the waters. The waters below are called the seas, oceans, and lakes. The sea will never roar. If it does, what could it be? Look at the word *expanse*. It means the unbroken surface of the sky. Who are the waters above? How are they connected to the sky? Man is seated in heavenly places. God set them there before they were born. Their spirit will dominate the atmosphere. What is God looking for? God is Spirit. His Spirit will live in man. Adam cannot eat the forbidden fruit. It will release the beast in the land. This raises one question: what happens when the spirit of the beast is released in the land? Read on as I give you the answer.

God's fatherhood will be destroyed. The waters will come down. This is the beginning of the Jezebel spirit. The globe will soon be drowned. These are the things God did not want. That is why they could not eat from the tree. God's Spirit wants to rule in man. God just wanted a family. The family became lustful and greedy. Judgment is in the land. This judgment is not from God. It is the judgment caused by man.

I will show you the pattern of the third day. Then I will reveal to you the waters. Remember, God closed the door before Adam was born. The family let Jezebel into the waters. This is the spirit of the lion. I will show what happens when the two get together, Jezebel and the lion. You will see the waters roar.

Genesis 1:9–10 reads, "And God said, Let the waters under the heaven be gathered together unto one place, and let the dry land appear: and it was so. And God called the dry land Earth; and the gathering together of the waters called he Seas: and God saw that it was good." This is the third day

God's Spirit is moving below. The waters below are put in place. God is looking at the dry land. I am sure He was thinking about His face. Look what He called the waters. The waters below are called "the seas." What could make this water roar? What is the definition for *sea*?

The Hebrew word for seas is *yam* (yawm), *Strong's* reference number 3220. It refers to any large body of water, often which may have waves that crash and roar. Look at the definition. This is the third day, you see. God did not want the waters to roar like a lion. They will never bother me. That is why He separated the waters. He put the firmament in between. Remember the waters have a face. I told you a pounding heart will beat. The waters above will follow man. The waters below are called the sea. The waters above are alive. They will never kill humanity. This water is connected to man. It will follow the face in the ground. God forbid the face to sin. If it does, the globe will drown.

I will show you more about the water. What do the waters have to do with the waters? God gave Adam a tree. Stay tuned until next time. I am revealing the mystery. Prophetess Juanita, continue to stand! Bishop Weeks, you are chosen by God. In my vision, you were combing the prophetess's hair. What does this mean to God? Her hair is her glory. Fight for the beauty that God sees. Your words will restore her beauty. She is every woman you see. Your pain is the pain of eternity. The heavens are now groaning. God is looking at the waters around you. I hear the waters moaning.

No more sheets! No more lust. I do not want it, God, I want love! I want passion. Give it to me, God. This is the cry of the waters. Who could the waters be? They are waiting in the firmament. Their hearts are pounding, you see. This is the heart of God. The waters are alive. The waters need the face of man. Their passion is speaking loud. I have a purpose and a plan! I belong to God. To whom is this water screaming out? I need a face, God!

Their hearts are beating in the firmament. Love continues to pound. Love is crying, "Don't leave me in lust. If you do, somebody will drown." God is calling for every man. You are the face of God. Your life will change the course of the waters. Now give your lives to God.

These are my final questions: who or what is this water? Why are heaven and earth passing away? Why is the globe drowning?

Now, here are my closing remarks. These rules are for everyone who is married, remarried, single, or divorced. They address issues on the children that may or may not be in the same house with you. These instructions will be for men and women. It does not matter if you are a married man with children by another woman or women. You might be a single man with several children by different women and are now born again. Perhaps you are the female that has the children and are married to someone that is not their biological father. Maybe you are the woman with the children and are not married at this time. If you live by the principles I am about to give you, you will never be ensnared or disappointed while doing the things that God requires of parents.

**Rule #1**

The number one rule for any man should be, "I am God's man, first." This will provoke you to be accountable to your wife. It will keep you from being tricked. You will be able to operate as a man of God and a father to your children. Most of all, nobody has to get hurt. Accountability to your spouse is designed to challenge your faith, build your trust, and strengthen your marriage. Many men want to answer to and be accountable only to God. This is why they sin repeatedly and repent privately.

These men answer to no one but themselves. They have not embraced the help that God wanted a man to have from his own wife. This raises one question to the single man: who are you accountable to?

**Rule #2**

You are the children's father and not their mother's man. This is very important for men to understand. God holds you responsible for your children. You are obligated to pray for them. God does not want your children to suffer. You need to pay your child support on time. As for visitation, that is something you and your wife should discuss together. Preparing a plan and having accountability will keep you from being seduced as a man.

**Rule #3**

Let's call it food for a man's thoughts. This rule says, "God sees me at all times. I am naked before Him. When I fail to communicate with my spouse, then both of us get hurt by the other spirit." It also means the other spirit leaves something on you both that will separate you from each other and God. This rule is born out of Genesis the first and second chapters.

God put the man in authority. The man failed to communicate with his wife. The serpent deceived the woman. He used her to seduce her own husband. The spirit of seduction continues today. It is operating in many women. Greed and deception are overthrowing the family. Our men are a product of what the first woman did.

Once again I say, beware of the serpent. He has now taken on a human form. This spirit is using women to seduce men who fail to communicate with the woman who is in the house with him. This raises one question: what is the serpent spirit using men to do to women?

You should know the answer to that. The globe is filled with men who are fighting lust and are angry. We have called them animals. Once again, we cannot just blame them. A woman must choose to be covered by the man.

The first woman ran out of the will of God. Her own desires became a direct attack against her. She did wrong and her husband agreed with it. Once again, men and women have failed to help each other. We are now in the final stage. God is declaring no more.

**Rule #4**

I will not be manipulated! The first woman was manipulated by the serpent. The serpent discussed something with her that her husband should have talked to her about. Even worse, he was talking to the woman while Adam was standing there. This same spirit operates in men and women. It will seduce your spouse while you are looking. Many times your spouse may stand there and ignore it.

Manipulation and seduction are deadly. Men and women must arm themselves to stand against these two spirits. This means a man should beware when his wife warns him about another woman. Likewise, the woman should allow her husband to minister to her in the same manner. This raises two questions: how was the woman manipulated by the serpent? What did he say to her while Adam just stood there? Read Genesis 3 to see the entire dialogue.

**Rule #5**

I should not be offended when my spouse warns or corrects me for my own good. This is very important. Many men have children that result from an affair. This at least causes his wife not to trust him, if not to end their marriage outright. Repentance and forgiveness are only part of the process. Accountability and communication are the things that will get her to trust you again. Many men often say, "You don't trust me." Yet, he does not understand the attack and the torment that his wife experiences in her mind because of the infidelity. Lack of accountability only causes her to feel like you have something to hide.

On the other hand, the husband may very well be innocent and really want to regain her trust. You must help her trust you, which means you must become accountable. Fighting for trust and refusing to be accountable will only leave you frustrated. You will never get the trust back that you forfeited if you allow pride and self-righteousness to make you feel like she ought to trust you when you refuse to be accountable. This raises a question: do married women have affairs? If so, why? Remember, God is not making an excuse for it!

**Rule #6**

I am the mother of his children, only—I am not his wife. This is something every woman must remember if they have children by a man that is not their husband or they are no longer married to. If he wants counsel, guide him to another brother, but do not try to counsel him yourself. Many times, women find themselves being seduced by a man that they have children by. At the same time, men have been seduced by women that they have children by. The man's goal was to stop by and visit the children. But he ignored all of the warnings that were always present each time he showed up. This pride has led to behavior that he now regrets.

Lust cannot be satisfied and pride always values its own opinion. Most of all, lust and pride always refuse correction while leaving your inner person screaming privately. Lust and pride bind the emotions and snatch a person's will. Although the person wants help, he does not get it because he thinks he knows how to help himself. This person must be broken by God. This means you will cry hard and long until you received God's way of escape. His way tells a man that he needs the help of his mate. At the same time, your mate needs your assistance. Your wife's ministry toward you is not designed to make her the dominant one. She is just a picture of the wisdom that God pulled out of you. God placed her in your life to keep you from falling in love with yourself and always valuing your own opinion. Together you are complete if you learn to submit and receive ministry from each other.

**Rule #7**

I will not allow my children to disrespect the man I married. They may never call him "Dad," but they will respect him as long as they are under our roof. This rule is a tough one. Many times, a woman might have several children by several men. Some of the children may be teenagers, which can sometimes be a challenge. She eventually becomes born again and God gives her a husband. This will be a test for her and the children. Are they ready to be covered by a man of God? Will the man be honored as the head? Or, will the man have to wrestle with the spirit of their biological father, which is now working in the children?

These are things that should be discussed before marriage. A single woman should nurture her children with her wisdom. She has the power to cultivate the soil of their souls and prepare them to desire a father. She cannot do that spending her days telling them how low down their dad is and how he does not love them. All of these things will release a harvest back toward her that she will not want to reap. She is one of many women God is watching. He will never release a new man to love or trust her when that man would be subject to getting hurt because she was not yet healed.

Nurture your children with your wisdom. Most of all, do not say another word that is negative about their dad. Maybe he did not treat you right, but he is still their father.

**Rule #8**

Your children deserve an inheritance. This is very challenging. Many children have been left in the wilderness. They are left with their mother. They may or may not know their biological fathers. God forbid a man to live large and then declare that God will take care of his children as if God is dropping money out of the sky. Many men are not hurting at all, financially. Yet, they have children who suffer.

Men, your children hate God and have even called you a hypocrite. They say it only because they often go to bed hungry and have raggedy clothes. It is not easy for men who are married or remarried and have children in another house. Sometime the check is in the mail and the mother of your child uses it inappropriately. On the other hand, she may have other children in her house and will use the money to run her house trying to make ends meet. However, you should set up a trust fund for your child and present it when he or she becomes an adult.

This next thing I speak with the compassion of God at hand. Yet, I say to the men, you are not obligated to do this. If a man of God's finances allows him, he should give a peace offering to the woman that has his children. This is a one-time peace offering, especially if she is poor. Many women have been used and left struggling. At the same time, many of the same women have seduced men and have aggressively come after any man for money. Yes, you are putting the check in the mail. You are obligated to do that. However, if your finances allow, give a one-time peace offering to the woman who had your children. Make sure if you do this, that it is something that your present wife agrees with. You do not want her to look at the checkbook and wonder what in the world you are up to. Also if you are getting married, share this book with your fiancé. Most of all, develop a plan together with how you will deal with the children that both of you may have by other people. When you fail to plan, then you plan to fail. Once again, it is all about communication and using God's principles.

This brings me to the last two questions. Earlier in this chapter I asked, where did darkness go once Adam sinned? Then I asked the single men who are they accountable to? I will talk about the single man at another time. In the meantime pray. Now I will answer the question about darkness. I will do it by showing you the first day of Creation again. This is how the globe actually looks now. Water is taking over. God's Spirit needs a face. Adam has already sinned. God has no place. Darkness is in authority. These spirits live in man. Sin broke down the firmament. Water is everywhere. Sin continually rules. A shaking is going on. God lives in eternity. There is a fight over the thrown. The serpent has taken over. This spirit lives in man. Lust opened the door to darkness. Now darkness lives in men. Here is the scripture. I have already explained it. This is how the globe is beginning to look. God's Spirit is present. He needs a body to operate through. Darkness and light need to be separate. Water is everywhere. God is looking for His face. The bishop and prophetess are the beginning of a new season in the globe. I love both of you! God, please show me Your face!

In the beginning God created the heaven and the earth. And the earth was without form, and void; and darkness was upon the face of the deep. And the Spirit of God moved upon the face of the waters. And God said, Let there be light: and there was light. And God saw the light, that it was good: and God divided the light from the darkness.

—Genesis 1: 1–4

TO CONTACT THE AUTHOR

alesiatwilliams@yahoo.com